FARMING THE LORD'S LAND

FARMING THE LORD'S LAND

Christian Perspectives on American Agriculture

Edited by Charles P. Lutz

AUGSBURG Publishing House • Minneapolis

Contents

* Discussion helps at the close of each chapter are
written by Victoria P. Oshiro.

The Manner of U.S. Farming

Foreword

Every decade probably seems a time of change to the people who live through it. Even so, the '70s have been a period of particularly significant transition for U.S. agriculture.

Ten years ago, the traditional farm problem seemed unsolved and all but unsolvable. We had almost started to think of overproduction and surpluses as a way of life. Then came the Russian grain deal and a roller coaster ride of up-and-down prices that disrupted the whole farm sector. We learned overnight what a fine line separates surplus from scarcity.

One of the most significant accomplishments of the last 10 years has been our success in restoring some order to agriculture. The farmer-held grain reserve, inaugurated with the 1977 Farm Bill, has shown its worth by providing a degree of stability to farming that allows producers to plan ahead and protects consumers from the worst consequences of chaotic markets.

Rising worldwide demand for U.S. farm products will create good markets during the coming decade. But I see some serious problems that we need to be considering right now. For one thing, the cost of farm inputs—especially fossil fuels—will continue to rise, cutting profit margins and imposing new burdens on producers. In addition, we can be much less certain from now on about what will happen on a year-to-year basis than we were, say, during the 1950s and 1960s. Some years will probably see a temporary return of surpluses. In other cases, there will be plenty of demand for everything we can produce. We need to refine programs and policies that will allow our farmers to respond rapidly to either set of circumstances.

I have a feeling that the technological revolution that has shaped agriculture since World War II may be ending. Declines in farm numbers and increases in farm size are both slowing. Productivity increases are slowing as well.

If the technological revolution is, in fact, drawing to a close, it means that we will not be able to count automatically on new machines, fertilizers, or crop varieties to boost production and cut costs in the future.

That, in turn, means that we will have to give increasing attention to other factors that influence agriculture's performance. Foremost among these is the way farming's productive resources are organized and controlled—what economists call farm *structure*.

I am trying to generate debate on this topic, partly in preparation for the 1981 Farm Bill, but also because it is an issue that I think will require serious deliberation for a long time to come.

Our margin for error will be much slimmer in the 1980s than it has been in the past. I want us to get ahead of the curve in terms of agricultural policy, to anticipate what is coming at us, rather than simply reacting to what has already hit us. We should start considering now where the farm sector is headed and what we can do to help prepare it for the future.

I therefore welcome this book as a significant contribution to our national deliberation. It is a fine book and I congratulate all of those responsible for its preparation.

BOB BERGLAND
United States Secretary of Agriculture

Editor's Introduction

This book came about for several reasons.

First, it has begun to dawn on many people that certain trends in U.S. agriculture, once viewed as solutions to earlier problems, have turned into problems themselves. Included would be the trends toward bigger and fewer farms, toward high technology and low labor, toward one-crop production on many farms, and toward heavy dependence on petroleum-based inputs. It seemed to me that a book on these concerns, in popular language and from a social ethics perspective, would be of some value to farmers and nonfarmers alike.

Second, converging with certain questions about the way we farm, there is a growing emphasis in both the church and other segments of our society on the care of the earth and its resource base, on the need for gentler and more care-filled nurturing of this fragile planet, on what Christians call "stewardship" of creation.

Third, in the course of nearly six years of experience with educational efforts on world food concerns, it has become clear to me that the future of farming in the United States and the world's future ability to meet its food needs are tied closely together.

Finally, in those years of working with food and farm issues, I have come across a number of people who were able to articulate clearly the nature of these ethical issues and what we might do about them. Why not invite a group of them to contribute to a book that would collect their concerns and insights?

This is the book that has resulted.

It is organized in three parts. Two chapters look at the relationships between U.S. farming and the food needs of people, globally and domestically. Four chapters then explore questions related to the *structure* of U.S. agriculture. A final four examine issues involved with the *manner* in which we farm.

All are keynoted by a special foreword written by Bob Bergland, a farmer who has been U.S. secretary of agriculture since 1977. Bergland served in the U.S. House of Representatives for six years prior to joining the President's cabinet, and during part of that time (1975-76) he was a member of the Task Force on World Hunger of the American Lutheran Church.

Two of the authors are currently farming. Several others have farm experience in their background. Three are present or former teachers of agriculture at the university level. One is a farm journalist. One is a former state commissioner of agriculture. All have a commitment to the survival of family-farm agriculture in the United States, though they might differ in defining what that should be.

Though none of the contributors read what the others were saying, in advance of their own writing, I think the essays complement one another. There is a variety of perspectives, but a clear consensus as well.

This book is intended for both farm and non-farm readers. The production of food and fiber, the care of soil and water, the survival of rural communities—these are obviously of importance to more than just the four percent of the U.S. population who live on farms.

I hope this book will be useful in discussion groups, within urban as well as rural settings, in churches and in community groups. (I thank Victoria Oshiro of the Hunger Action Coalition/Minnesota for developing the discussion helps.)

I am not a farmer. But I was reared in rural communities in northern Iowa, where some of the world's most productive farming takes place. I worked on the farms of relatives and neighbors for many summers. The experience of living and working there initiated in me the growth of a profound gratitude for the blessing that U.S. agriculture has been under God—to those who farm and to those who live from what is produced on our land.

People who do not farm often see farming as simply another economic activity, another way of making a living. It is that. But it is also much more. It is a way of life. It is a life that provides the chance to see firsthand and up-close how we all depend on the planet's resource base, God's creation.

I first learned the word *stewardship* in that context—care of the earth, recycling of life-giving substances, carefull management of what has been provided, and rhythmic working in harmony with nature's cycles. I first learned of stewardship in the setting of farming, before I heard it used in the much narrower sense of raising or managing money for the church.

Along with the discussion of problems or ethical questions, I believe this book conveys some of the wonder of being God's co-creators, which farmers are in a special way.

If you do not farm, I hope that reading this book will convey a bit of the awesome privilege and responsibility which is the calling of farmers.

If you do farm, I hope this book will be a new reminder of that wondrous gift which God has given in allowing you to be a tender of his vineyard. It is indeed the Lord's land that you farm. And through your farming of it, God has a way of loving both you and your neighbor.

CHARLES P. LUTZ
harvest season 1979

1

U.S. Farming and World Food Needs

by Charles P. Lutz[*]

There's more to world hunger and domestic hunger than the ability of farmers to produce. Hunger is more than a food question. It's a distribution question. It's a sociological question. It's a question of education . . . a question of systems. That is why we are going to have to become a great deal more sophisticated in solving hunger at home and abroad than just assuming that if we can produce, that automatically solves the problem.

JOHN WHITE
Deputy U.S. Secretary of Agriculture

[*] CHARLES P. LUTZ is coordinator of the hunger program of the American Lutheran Church and director for global education in the ALC's Division for Life and Mission in the Congregation. A journalist and writer on numerous topics in the area of the church's social witness, he is the editor of this book.

The chief problem for much of the world the rest of this century will be simply *to get enough to eat.*

The chief problem for many farmers in the United States, today and in the years just ahead, will be *to survive as farm operators.*

There's a connection between these two problems.

For one thing, U.S. farmers produce food not only for Americans but also for millions of other people around the world, both rich and poor. The other side of that coin is that much of our agricultural economy depends on the health of the global economy, the ability of food consumers elsewhere to buy the food we have to sell.

This chapter seeks to put in global context the situation of farming in the United States. We will examine first some fallacies concerning our nation and world food needs. Next, we will explore the continuing dilemma of U.S. agriculture: bountiful production and inadequate prices. Finally, I will suggest some policy goals for our society in relation to agriculture, the broad strokes of which receive the general support of most religious groups in our country today.

U.S. Food and World Needs: Four Fallacies

There are a number of misunderstandings in the popular mind about our food production and the world's food needs. We will examine four of them here.

Fallacy 1: "The United States is the world's breadbasket." If this statement means to suggest that the United States produces a major portion of the world's food, or even its grains, it is incorrect. It's hard to be precise about global food production, since much of it never gets counted precisely. But the best estimates run something like the following:

In grains (wheat, rice and feed grains) the estimate is that the U.S. produces about 13% of the annual world production. In wheat production, the Soviet Union leads

the world almost every year. In rice, China produces
more than anybody else.

But it is also true that the U.S. leads all the major
producing nations in production of grains *per capita*.
Further, we export more grains than anybody else.

Of all the grains produced in a current year, about
one bushel in every eight moves internationally, and
roughly 60% of that amount originates in the United
States. Thus, about 7% of the planet's annual grain production is represented by what we export from our farmlands to other nations.

So we are important, the most important grain-export-
ing nation, in fact. But it is also true that most of the
world's peoples produce most of their own food most of
the time. They are their *own* breadbasket. That's a more
accurate comment about the world's poor nations than
about the world's higher-income countries. The poor of
the earth are, in very high percentage, engaged in subsistence agriculture. They grow their own food or they
don't eat.

And poor countries, for the most part, can't afford to
buy large amounts of food in the world market. In fact,
many of them *export* food and other agricultural products to the rich countries. Things like coffee, tea, cocoa,
bananas, jute, and sisal—and even sugar, soybeans, and
beef—are produced and shipped out to earn foreign exchange with which to buy manufactured goods from industrial nations like the U.S.

Yes, the U.S. exports a lot of food. Our export total
in agricultural products (including some non-food
items) was $32 billion in 1979. But about two-thirds of
that agricultural export goes to other industrial nations,
including both capitalist and socialist economies (see
Table 1).

The United States imports a substantial volume of
food also. We don't import as much as we ship out, but
our agricultural imports have run about 50%-60% of
our agricultural exports in recent years.

While we're very important in world food trade, as both an exporter and importer, it's hardly accurate to refer to us as "the world's breadbasket."

Fallacy 2: "We provide massive food aid to the world." Throughout the 1970s, U.S. food aid averaged only about 4% of our total food export. It's true that it was much higher, once upon a time. In the late 1950s and early 1960s, when we had large surpluses of grain that could not find buyers in the world market, we sometimes sent as much as 20%-25% of our grain exports in the form of food aid. But our food aid today is relatively small, as a percentage of our exports.

It should also be understood that the bulk of our food aid is not a gift and never has been. It is usually offered on a long-term loan basis, or at a discounted rate, below

Table 1. U.S. Farm Exports in Billions of Dollars

	1975	1976	1977	1978	1979	*1979 pct.*
Developed market countries*	12.2	12.1	14.1	15.4	16.5	*51.5%*
Centrally planned countries**	1.5	3.3	2.1	2.6	4.7	*14.7%*
Developing countries***	8.2	7.2	7.8	9.4	10.8	*33.8%*
totals	21.9	22.6	24.0	27.3	32.0	*100.0%*

*Western Europe, Canada, Japan, Oceania

**USSR, Eastern Europe, China

***Latin America, Africa, Asia (excluding Japan and China)

the world market price. The only food aid that is given away is the relatively small portion which is channeled through voluntary agencies, such as Lutheran World Relief, in emergency situations.

There continues to be a need for food aid from the U.S. and other countries that are in a position to extend it—to meet emergency needs. But it is generally considered a good thing that our food aid is not as large a program as it was a couple decades ago. The reasons are basically two:

1. Food aid in large amounts and extended over a number of years proved to be a disincentive to the farm sectors of recipient nations' economies. It led a number of low-income countries into a false sense of security, so that they did not give proper attention to developing their own agriculture.

2. Aid in forms *other than food* can be far more useful in assisting development. Technical assistance and funds for building agricultural infrastructures can normally do more to help poor countries with their own food production.

So as a people we can and should do more in development assistance within low-income nations, but the proportion that goes in the form of food is now very small. And that's a good thing.

Fallacy 3: "U.S. farmers are heavily subsidized by the federal taxpayer." Subsidies in the form of payments supporting commodity prices totaled $2 billion in 1978, the largest amount since 1973. Nearly half went to the 10% of farm program participants who operate the largest farms. In contrast, the smaller 50% of the farms received only 10% of the payments. In recent years dairy producers have probably had the best price-support situation, and grain and meat producers much less.

Federal help to farmers in the form of tax advantages has tended also to favor the few large operations much more than the many middle-size and small farms. Most of the farm tax advantages are also available to other kinds of businesses.

Overall, American farmers receive far less in government supports than the producers of most industrial nations. The farmers of the European Common Market, for example, are much more sheltered from fluctuations in world market prices than are American farmers.

Further, many U.S. farmers in recent years have been rich in net worth but poor in cash flow. That is, they have substantial assets in land and equipment, but they have a hard time providing for their families from current income. Some have said they can be well-off only by quitting, or by dying.

Fallacy 4: "Farm prices are the main determiner of food prices, and food prices are too high." There are two distinct parts to this statement: (1) the role of farm prices in determining food prices, and (2) food price levels.

Food prices are made up of the farm value (what the farmer gets) and the marketing cost (what various middle persons get). The farm value is what the producer is paid for the raw agricultural commodities. The marketing value is everything else that goes into what consumers pay in retail stores.

For meat, poultry, and dairy products, the farm value is more than half the retail price. But for most grain and fruit and vegetable products, the reverse is true. What the farmer receives may run as high as 70% or as low as 10% of the retail price. (In mid-1978, when wheat prices were low, wheat farmers got only 8% of the price of a loaf of bread, while cattle farmers were receiving 62% of the average price of a pound of beef.)

Overall, in the late 1970s, farmers were receiving about one dollar of every three we consumers spent in food markets, with the other two dollars going to processors, packagers, transporters, advertisers, wholesalers, retailers, and whoever else had a piece of the food marketing business.

Further, most of the increase in food costs in the past decade has been in the marketing sector, not the farm-value portion. In fact, often during the past decade the prices of food in the stores would be rising while the prices received by farmers were falling!

The second part of the statement that food prices are "too high" depends on the answer to the question, "Compared to what?" One accepted way of measuring food costs is as a percentage of income. Certainly, for people on limited income and for the poor in America, the current prices of food are too high. That's one reason our society provides both income assistance and direct food assistance to low-income people (see Chapter 2).

But taken as a proportion of average family income in the U.S., we have the world's *least* expensive food. It amounts to about 17% of the average family income in this country, meaning five dollars in six are available for purposes other than feeding ourselves. This percentage compares to an estimated 21%-25% in Western Europe and Japan, and an estimated 35% in the Soviet Union. Are prices in the U.S. too high compared to what other peoples pay? Or too high compared to what we're used to?

Sometimes our sense of what is right and fair in consumer prices leads to odd conclusions. A 50-cent cup of soda pop at a ball game is acceptable, but a 20-cent glass of milk for breakfast is considered inflationary. And $5 for a ticket to a movie is okay, but $3.50 for a bushel of wheat is too high. And cotton at 65¢ a pound is steep but a $20 shirt is a bargain when on sale for $18.50.

Many observers believe that food prices in the United States are actually too low and need to increase—in order for our farmers to receive a fair return for their labor and a more equitable share of national income. The problem is finding a way to assure that future food price increases benefit the farmer rather than further increasing the income of all the post-farm handlers.

The Production/Price Squeeze

Food consumers, here at home and overseas, have benefited from the high productivity per worker-hour of American agriculture and the relatively low prices that have resulted. But our producers have suffered through periods of low prices caused by overproduction.

It's been impossible to find a solution to the high production/low price problem that is acceptable to both farmers and consumers. Various farm programs have been tried during the past 50 years. Some form of governmental protection against disastrously low prices—coupled with an agreement to control production, and allowing individual farmers the option of participating —appears to be the best compromise policy. This is basically the program our country currently has. A revision of the federal farm program in 1981 will build on what has been in place, and there is strong agitation to reverse the *direction* of government assistance, toward more help to smaller and moderate-size farmers.

At present, farm program assistance gives more support to the larger operators, usually on the simple basis that they produce more. Many observers now believe that public support for farming should be skewed toward the smaller operators, with an actual cut-off in benefits once an operation reaches a certain volume of production.

To return to the global context, the cost/price squeeze experienced by U.S. farmers is similar to the economic problem facing many Third World countries which export primary commodities. They and U.S. farmers have three realities in common:

1. Both produce a primary commodity, a raw material. (For low-income countries, it may be agricultural products—either food or fiber—or it may be an extracted commodity such as bauxite or copper.)

2. Both depend on taking the price offered by the world market, a price they cannot set (sellers of pro-

cessed goods can, to a degree), and which fluctuates un-
predictably. The price may be affected by weather, if
the product is agricultural, or it may be affected by
isolated decisions about production among countless producers, or it may be affected by consumers' shifting needs
or desires for the product.

3. Both watch helplessly as someone else benefits from
the value added through processing or transporting or
distributing their product. In the case of wheat farmers,
for example, their raw material gives jobs and dependable income to truckers and shippers, bakers and advertisers, grain companies and food processors, wholesalers
and retailers. In the case of low-income countries, their
raw materials bring jobs and dependable income to the
industrialized countries in the Northern Hemisphere:
factories, stockholders, workers, shipping companies, and
distributors.

The wheat in a 50¢ loaf of bread brings about 4¢ to
the farmer. Raw materials from the low-income countries
which brought them $30 billion in a recent year sold
to the eventual consumer in the high-income countries
for $200 billion. The final $170 billion (85% of the retail total) accrued to workers and economies *outside*
the producing countries. In either case, most of the
money is made *after* the raw material leaves the farmer's
gate or the Southern Hemisphere port. Yet nearly all
the price risk is taken by the producer of the primary
commodity.

So U.S. farmers do know something of what it means
to be economically dependent, like Third World peoples.
Both are asking for a kind of *parity* or *equity* in economic return.

What is fair and needed for Third World countries
is a shift in the global patterns of labor, so that they may
be encouraged and enabled to employ more of their
own people in processing their own raw materials. This
will mean lowering our protective trade barriers and al-

lowing into our markets processed goods made and shipped by low-income countries.

What is fair and needed for U.S. farmers is assurance that they will get reasonable benefit from the food raw materials they produce. This means policies that at least help to keep smaller farmers in business when prices are low—policies that balance price supports with production controls, that reward farmer incentive and wise stewardship of the land and water resource base.

Some Policy Goals for Our Society

There are several broad goals for U.S. public policy in relation to agriculture that are generally supported by farm organizations, religious groups, and those who have a special concern for the world food situation. In summary form, I see these goals as five basic points:

1. Give family farming a chance to survive as the basic social and economic unit of rural America. (The definition of a family farm which is used in this book is one developed by the Interreligious Task Force on U.S. Food Policy: "An agricultural production unit in which the management, economic risk, and most of the labor—peak seasons excepted—are provided by a given family and from which that family receives the bulk of its earnings. Family farms can range from a one-acre tobacco allotment in North Carolina to a Kansas wheat spread of several thousand acres. It is defined not in terms of acreage but of independent entrepreneurship." [2])

In 1945 the U.S. had 5.9 million farms. In 1979 there were roughly 2.6 million (2.3 million counting those with sales of $1000 and above). If current trends continue, by the year 2000 we will have only 1.6 million. Even with substantial revision in traditional farm policy, to favor survival of smaller farmers, it is estimated that we will still be down to 2 million farms by the year 2000.

The labor force on our present 2.6 million farms is

calculated at 4 million people, or less than 4% of the
national work force. The total population living on
farms is also under 4% today.

The implications of this decline in farming population—and some ways of slowing it—are discussed in more
detail later in this book. The point here is that most
students of the problem believe a further decline in farm
population would have negative consequences for our
society, as well as for those who wish to continue farming, and our national policy should be to encourage
continuation of a family-farm structure of agriculture.
(See especially Chapters 3, 4 and 6.)

2. *Maintain a high level of food production,* consistent
with sound stewardship practices. This goal is based on
the assumption that the world will need all the food
that can be rationally produced, and to let fertile acres
lie unfarmed for long would be a mistake.

During years when more food is produced than can
be absorbed in the marketplace by current needs, we
should put food into reserves. We have begun in the
U.S. with a domestic reserve program for grains, held by
farmers, basically for price-stabilization reasons. We
should also develop reserves for international emergency
purposes, in which many countries would be participating. And we could help food-deficit nations build up
their own reserves of grain by giving them assistance
during our own years of excess production.

There are ways of encouraging full production (always
consistent with good management of our resource base)
without cutting the economic heart out of our farmers'
livelihood.

3. *Provide a financial floor for farmers,* an assured minimum price below which they will not have to fall. It
need not be an assured profit, but it probably should
be at the level of production costs. These vary substantially from farm to farm, and it is therefore impossible
to come up with a formula that fits everyone.

Even though we are dealing in rough national averages, I think it is fair that our society promise farmers they will recover their production costs, even in the worst of years. Others, of course, including a fair number of farmers, may disagree. One of the tougher points in this debate is how to figure the cost of land, which should be counted a part of production costs. Should land be valued at the original purchase price or at current market value?

I agree with those who say that not all the risk should be removed from farming. But can we not cushion the impact of disastrously low prices, so that more farmers may survive the lean years and be around to benefit from the fat ones?

4. Develop wise, future-oriented policies of water and land use, as well as policies of land tenure that encourage farms to be passed from generation to generation in the same family, and policies that restrain loss of land to non-farm uses.

The issues here are both environmental stewardship and encouragement of dispersed ownership. Usually when farms cannot be passed from parents to their children they are acquired by neighboring farms, either whole or in pieces, and the neighboring operators simply become larger.

5. Strengthen all aspects of rural community, including education, health services, housing, transportation, and all the amenities of life. This concern is the subject of Chapter 6.

How Can Churches Help Pursue Such Goals?

The primary role of church bodies in developing a coherent U.S. social policy concerning agriculture is in the area of *education.* Churches have within their membership both farmers and nonfarmers. It is the latter who need the greater help, educationally, regarding farm policy. Church bodies can serve as convenors of groups that include both farm and non-farm members, for dialog on farm and food policy concerns.

In addition, churches can sometimes be convenors of farmers who have a variety of policy viewpoints. In farm organizations they tend to gather according to particular political or economic philosophies, or in special commodity groupings. When a church has farmers of varied philosophies in its membership, it offers a genuine service by bringing them together for discussion of the broad policy questions that are a concern to the larger society. The church is also a logical convenor of groups that include both consumers and producers of food.

Finally, the churches have a role in shaping public policy. They can encourage their members to become informed participants in the legislation-building process. (See the Resources section of this book for information on public-policy groups.) Sometimes church bodies themselves will take official stands on particular policy questions.

The churches have always been known for their encouragement of voluntary sharing of food with the hungry. Today they are also called to promote justice in the world's systems of food and food production. That means becoming political, and intelligently helping to shape humane farm and food policies—without abandoning voluntary sharing. In terms of both hungry people around the world and U.S. farmers, it means dealing with what is right and just and fair, as well as with what is merciful.

Notes

1. U.S. Department of Agriculture, *Farmers Newsletter* (September 1979).
2. Interreligious Task Force on U.S. Food Policy, Washington, D.C., "Family Farming and the Common Good," Hunger No. 7 (February 1977).

For Discussion

1. An introductory exercise mainly for nonfarmers: What are your visions of farms and farming? Share these visions in the group. Do you think the *kinds* of farms we have (size, who manages them, how they are farmed) makes any difference to urban people? Why or why not?

2. How significant are U.S. farm exports to our economy? What does the relative size of the numbers in the chart below say about our economic relationships with the rest of the world—with the *developing* countries? What would you want to see changed in these figures? If changes were made, who in our economic life would be affected?

	billions of dollars (est.)
1979 U.S. exports (all countries, all products)	180.0
1979 U.S. farm exports	32.0
1979 U.S. farm exports to developing countries	10.8
1979 U.S. food aid (gifts)	0.4
(sold on concessional terms)	0.8
1979 total of U.S. overseas development assistance (including food)	5.9

3. As a nation we apply revenue from our exports toward the cost of our imports. List the imported agricultural products (food, beverages, fibers) that you use. What other imported products do you depend on?

4. Farm price-support payments in 1978 totaled about $2 billion. The federal share of the school breakfast and lunch program was roughly the same figure. Can you think of direct benefits to others from federal subsidies? Are you buying a house with federal assistance (federally insured loan, tax credit for interest on home mortgage payments)? Do you drive on federally financed highways? Does your school get federal funds? Does your community have federal money for a sewage system or other municipal facility? Are farmers "heavily" subsidized?

5. For which foods do farmers get higher or lower percentages of the retail price? Why? What sort of consumer demands affect this? If we want a greater proportion of the

retail dollar to go to the farmer, how would it change the kinds of food we buy or the way we prepare food in our homes? How do you feel about such changes?

6. Food prices have increased in recent years. Has it caused any changes in your eating habits? For suggestions on how to eat nutritiously and more economically, consult the *More-with-Less Cookbook* by Doris Janzen Longacre (Herald Press, 1976). Your church group may want to have a potluck dinner or bake sale using recipes from this book, to help people see that they can indeed have more with less.

7. Julius Nyerere, president of Tanzania, has said that Third World nations are "price takers, not price makers." What does that statement mean for developing nations? Is it also true for U.S. farmers? How could each group work to become "price makers" for their commodities? What would such actions mean for others, both in the U.S. and in other nations?

8. Should U.S. policy encourage *family* farming? Why? Does it make any difference to city people? If we should encourage family farming with public policies (legislation), how would you do that? If we are not the world's breadbasket ("Fallacy 1"), why is it important to maintain a high level of food production?

9. The closing part of Chapter 1 talks about the role of churches. Do you agree with the suggestions? Have any of them been a part of your church life? Are there any you think your church should consider? Could you and others in your discussion group urge your congregation to engage in some of these activities?

2

U.S. Farmers and Our Public Food Programs

by Charles P. Lutz[*]

Congress further finds that increased utilization of food in establishing and maintaining adequate national levels of nutrition will promote the distribution in a beneficial manner of the nation's agricultural abundance and will strengthen the nation's agricultural economy, as well as result in more orderly marketing and distribution of foods.

From Congressional Declaration of Policy,
The Food Stamp Act of 1977

---

[*] CHARLES P. LUTZ has coordinated the world hunger program of the American Lutheran Church since January 1975. A frequent writer and speaker on social ethics and the Christian faith, he collected and edited the essays in this book.

There are hungry people in the United States. They are hungry not because of a lack of food in America, but because they are poor.

We have public programs designed to help the hungry in America. There are income-support programs and there are food programs. Most of the food programs are framed by the same committees in Congress that write the farm programs. The dollars to sustain most of the food programs are part of the budget of the U.S. Department of Agriculture.

So there is a connection between farm programs and food programs for the poor, between farm people and recipients of food assistance. And yet there is no real alliance between the two groups. Their "marriage" in federal legislation and administration is viewed as unnatural by both groups.

This chapter seeks to explore that relationship and to suggest that the two groups—farmers and low-income food aid recipients—need each other. The self-interest of each brings them together.

We begin with an outline of our domestic public food programs. Then there will be a discussion of what these programs mean to food producers, followed by a look at the politics of farm and food policy making.

A Survey of the Federal Food Programs

Public assistance—what is commonly called "welfare" —takes many forms in the United States. One important form of support is food assistance, provided through several programs funded by federal taxpayers.

These programs of assistance in the form of food (or money to buy food) have been funded at a level of almost $10 billion for the fiscal year 1980. What are the various programs and what do they accomplish? They fall into three categories. (The following material is summarized from data gathered by Bread for the World,

the Christian citizens movement on hunger and poverty.[1])

1. Food Stamps. By far the biggest hunger relief effort
is the program known as Food Stamps. It replaced an
earlier program in which food commodities were distributed directly. In late 1979 the program was serving
nearly 19 million people, almost one in 12 Americans.

Food stamps go to individuals or families, people who
buy and prepare food together. The value of the coupons
received depends on the combined income of the household and the number of people in it. The program uses
coupons issued by the Department of Agriculture, which
are administered by local offices under the supervision
of state social service departments.

The Food Stamp Program is actually an income-support program targeted to the purchase of food. To be
eligible, a family of four must have net income of less
than $596 a month. With *no* net income, a family of
four would receive up to $204 per month. But most fam-
ilies have some income and therefore receive less in
stamps. The program, as of late 1979, was transfering
nearly $7 billion in purchasing power on an annual
basis.

2. Child nutrition programs. These programs also are
administered by the Department of Agriculture. In fiscal
1980 they represent another $2 billion-plus. The chief
elements of the child nutrition programs are:

● *National School Lunch Program.* Launched in 1946
as a way of helping distribute surplus farm commodities,
in the past decade this program has given increased attention to the needs of poor children. Free or reduced-
price lunches grew to a $1.2 billion program serving
almost 12 million children by 1979. The government
spends another $600 million subsidizing in part the
lunches of all 26.5 million participants, including the
nonpoor.

● *School Breakfast Program.* This effort was begun as a pilot program in 1966 and given permanent status by Congress in 1975. More than three million children participate at an annual cost of $200 million.

● *Summer Food Service for Children.* This extends the school-lunch approach into summertime. More than 1.4 million low-income children received meals through parks and playgrounds in summer feeding during 1979.

● *Child Care Food Program.* Government-assisted meals served in day-care and after-school facilities, orphanages, homes for the handicapped, and other residential institutions for children reached 644,000 children in 1979.

● *Women, Infants and Children Special Program.* The awareness of the importance of good nutrition during fetal development, infancy, and early childhood led Congress in 1972 to provide supplemental protein-rich food to nutritionally vulnerable pregnant and nursing women, infants, and young children. By 1979 it was serving nearly 1.5 million people at a cost of $550 million. The program provides not only food but also nutrition education for the mothers.

3. *Nutrition for the elderly.* There are two kinds of programs: in-home and group setting or congregate dining. The former, usually called "meals on wheels," is for persons who are shut-in. Congregate dining is for persons 60 years and older who can come together in a group setting, where social and educational enrichment are also possible.

Both kinds of programs are federally-funded but usually administered by private groups, often churches.

Food programs for the elderly are serving 2.3 million people (1979) and the $202 million budget item is managed by the Department of Health and Human Services.

What do all these food programs add up to in terms of combating hunger and poverty in our society? The

Field Foundation in 1979 published a study on the changes in the U.S. pattern of hunger and malnutrition over the previous decade. In summarizing their findings the Field medical research team wrote:

Our first and overwhelming impression is that there are far fewer grossly malnourished people in this country today than there were ten years ago. Malnutrition has become a subtler problem. . . . Even in areas which did not command national attention ten years ago, many poor people now have food and look better off. This change does not appear to be due to an overall improvement in living standards or to a decrease in joblessness in those areas. In fact, the facts of life for Americans living in poverty remain as dark or darker than they were ten years ago. But in the area of food there is a difference. The Food Stamp Program, the nutritional component of Head Start, school lunch and breakfast programs . . . and WIC feeding programs have made the difference.[2]

The Field team also concluded that, while public food programs have made a major contribution to improving the health of the poor, they are still far from sufficient. The report says:

We are not dealing with an ineffective tool of public policy, but with an inadequately used one. Congress, the President, and the public should know that the very effectiveness of such programs, where they do work, makes it a greater national tragedy that many people remain unreached [by them].[3]

Food Programs and the Farm Economy

Our domestic food programs *do* work to help the poor get food—where they are being offered with proper outreach and education efforts. They are also a significant part of our federal budget: nearly $10 billion a year. If you include our overseas food assistance (Food for Peace), the total is more than $11 billion—and all of that provides jobs and income for people in our own U.S. economy. More than $4 billion of the total goes directly into the pockets of U.S. farmers in purchase of their production.

In fact, that is part of the legislative intent behind our food programs. The stated objectives in nearly every food program law include these two kinds of goals:

a. *to promote nutrition among the poor*
b. *to expand the demand for agricultural products*

It is not accidental that the second objective is written into the legislation.

Nearly 5% of all food purchased in the U.S. for home consumption is bought with food stamps. And our food aid that goes overseas is, of course, purchased from American farmers exclusively. Despite these obvious connections, American farmers have the same ambivalence about our food programs as the U.S. public in general, and at times it seems that some farm organizations express actual hostility. Why?

One apparent reason is the feeling among many farmers that "welfare" for the poor should not be a part of either the legislation or the Cabinet department which also deal with farming. Both domestic food programs and international food aid should be somewhere else than in the Department of Agriculture, according to this line of argument.

Another view, shared by many in Congress and also by a substantial number of food producers, is that the two kinds of legislation do indeed belong together. The argument here is that the politics of shaping farm and food legislation today require support from a variety of interest groups.

The Politics of Farm and Food

A kind of trade-off has developed in Congress over the past decade or so. Representatives of farm interests and those who speak for recipients of federal food programs have begun to work together. Neither group by itself

could achieve passage of the legislation it desired. So cooperation has become quite open and welcome to both sides.

Those whose primary constituency is farm people have declined in numbers. But two new kinds of representatives, primarily from urban districts, have come along and shown interest in legislation relating to food. One of these "new agenda" types is the congressperson who represents a substantial number of low-income people who benefit from federal food programs. The other is the congressperson who has a strong interest in the concerns of all food consumers—nutrition and food safety.

The so-called new-agenda representatives, backed by lobbying groups that are growing in strength, have done a number of things that affect farmers:

● They have sought and gained seats on agriculture committees of both houses in Congress.

● They have used those seats to help shape and provide support for new policy directions, such as the farmer-held grain reserves program enacted in 1977.

● They have gained a significant presence within the administrative halls of the Department of Agriculture.

● They have expanded to other constituencies the notion that there is trouble down on the farm. The nature of that trouble, as these new-agenda non-farm folk communicate it, includes both the economic problem of inadequate farm income and the societal problem of declining farm population.

Control of public food programs, domestic and international, has thus far remained with the Department of Agriculture and the congressional agriculture committees. My own view is that this is a good thing for farmers. My reasons are three:

1. Farmers need the support of non-farm members of Congress to get favorable farm legislation passed. (The reverse is also true, of course: the food programs need

support from representatives who do not have large concentrations of the poor.)

2. It helps non-farm populations to learn about and gain empathy for the situation of farmers. The widespread concerns about hunger in America and overseas have also provided some education about farming and farm economics in the United States. Farmers have been a major part of that process of educating the rest of us.

3. The alliance can remind both food producers and food-assistance recipients that they share a kind of economic vulnerability in our social system. The nature of the risk is different, but both face economic insecurities.

I don't know if these two groups—the hungry and those who grow food to feed the hungry—can ever be really comfortable together. I don't know if the "strange bedfellows" feeling can be overcome by either group.

There is one fascinating effort, though, in southwestern Wisconsin. There a project, launched by a farmer and involving Lutheran congregations that serve a large number of farmers in four counties, is doing outreach and education about the federal food programs. The effort has gathered church funds and hired a coordinator to reach the hungry with help and to educate others about the needs in their communities. One goal is to get the poor and non-poor residents of rural areas involved in one another's lives. (The project is sponsored by the Viroqua Conference of the American Lutheran Church; more information can be secured from ALC Viroqua Conference, Box 203, Soldiers Grove, Wisc. 54655.)

It's worth noting that in most of the developing world the poor and hungry *are* those who farm. The great majority of hungry people in the rest of the world are *rural* people, living on the land, but often not controlling the land they work. They are those who are said to be engaging in "subsistence agriculture," but most of the time they do not subsist very well. On this point the president of Tanzania, Julius Nyerere, said the following in a 1979 address to the World Conference on Agrarian Reform and Rural Development:

The root of world poverty, as well as the mass of it, lies in the rural areas. Urban poverty is more obvious—the slums and degradation of some towns in the developing countries force themselves upon the notice of the most casual visitor from other states. But the bulk of the slum inhabitants and the beggars on our streets have migrated to towns because they are pushed out of the rural areas by landlessness, joblessness, and hopelessness. . . .

An effective attack on world poverty can only be made by going direct to the rural areas and dealing with the problems there. . . . That objective can only be achieved if certain basic facts are recognized and acted upon. First among these is that those who own the land will use it for their own benefit. . . . If the land is owned by the peasants, either individually or collectively, it will be used to meet their needs. Actions which transfer land to the people are an essential first step in the fight against poverty. . . .

And even if effective land reform is carried out, that is not enough. The poor who have gained land under it—again whether privately or cooperatively—have to have access to credit, to improved seeds and tools, and to new knowledge, if the transfer of power over the land's resources is to be permanent and to lay the basis for future development. . . .

I repeat. Rural development means development. It indicates an approach, and the order of priorities. . . . it means acting to reverse the traditional flow of wealth from the rural areas into the towns and forcing that wealth into channels which will benefit the workers who actually produce it with their hands and their brains. It means transferring to the poorer and rural areas some of the wealth produced in the richest economic sectors. In practically all the developing countries these things require a revolution in the present patterns of government expenditure and of taxation. They will be done if, and only if, the people can organize their own power in their own interest. . . . Political power has to be exercised by the poor if the present flow of wealth towards wealth is to be stopped and the cooperative activities of man directed towards the abolition of poverty everywhere.[4]

Many of Dr. Nyerere's words apply to farm people and the rural sectors of the industrial world as well as to the developing nations. Note, for example, his point about the land being used to serve those who control it, or his insistence that the wealth produced in rural areas be permitted to stay in rural areas.

But there's also a difference. Many of the rural population in the U.S. are *not* poor. Can they identify with the impoverished and the hungry of our country?

To put the question another way: Is it possible that American farmers *can learn to like food stamps?* I hope so.

Not because farmers need to apply for food stamps, though there are many farming families whose annual incomes in certain years make them eligible for food stamp assistance.

And not because food stamps are the ideal solution to poverty. Jobs for those who can work and some form of guaranteed income security for those who cannot work would be better than food stamps. With food stamps we still depend basically on an approach of charity and paternalism.

But as long as we do rely on public food programs, food stamps will symbolize something in our society. And I wonder if farmers cannot learn to like food stamps as a symbol of a certain kind of society:

- a society that wants to help hungry people;
- a society that wants to give its farmers a fair deal;
- and a society in which food producers and the poorest of food consumers can work together to support one another.

Notes

1. *Bread for the World Newsletter* (November 1979).
2. Nick Kotz, "Hunger in America: the Federal Response," Field Foundation, New York, 1979.
3. Ibid.
4. Julius Nyerere, "On Rural Development," address delivered to the World Conference on Agrarian Reform and World Development, July 13, 1979, in Rome. Copies are available from Food and Agriculture Organization, North American Liaison Office, 1776 F St. NW, Washington, D.C. 20037.

For Discussion

1. Do you agree that farmers and low-income food consumers need each other? Why or why not?

2. A family of four with *no* income is allowed up to $204 per month in food stamps. Do you know how much your family spends on food each month?

3. How many of the public food programs described in this chapter are available in your community? Is your church involved in any of them?

4. There are studies of federal programs which indicate that some areas having the biggest payments to farmers also have the lowest proportions of eligible people taking part in federal food programs. What do you think that means?

5. Reread the quotations from the report of the Field medical research team on page 33. What in their conclusions is encouraging? What is discouraging? What have the federal food programs accomplished? What have they *not* accomplished?

6. Food stamps, including the cost of administering the program, cost taxpayers nearly $8 billion a year. The same amount of money keeps the U.S. military program running for about three weeks; it's less than the cost of five Trident submarines. Discuss the group's attitudes toward large expenditures for military and social welfare programs.

7. Poor people are found in the U.S. and in Third World countries such as Tanzania. Reread the quotation from President Nyerere. How is the situation he describes like that of poor people in the U.S.? How is it different?

8. "And I wonder if farmers cannot learn to like food stamps as a symbol of a certain kind of society." Doesn't this sentence apply to all people, not just farmers? Can *you* learn to like food stamps, even if you don't depend on them to eat?

THE STRUCTURE OF U.S. FARMING

3

Family Farming: Does It Serve the Common Good?

by Paul C. Johnson*

Those who will take time to investigate will clearly see that the issue isn't if but when small-scale agriculture will blossom in the U.S. The sooner the better—considering that small-scale agriculture can better cope with the rising cost and growing scarcity of fossil fuels, the growing scarcity of water, the urgent need to stop the alarming depletion rate of soil fertility by erosion, and stream pollution and other environmental degradation also caused by erosion, fertilizers and pesticides.

WILLIAM NORRIS
Chairman, Control Data Corporation
From *The Minneapolis Star,* August 30, 1979

* PAUL C. JOHNSON is a former editor of *Prairie Farmer* and associated farm magazines. He is a graduate of St. Olaf College, which honored him with a Doctor of Humane Letters degree in 1953. A country newspaper editor for 10 years, he also taught at the University of Minnesota's Institute of Agriculture for seven years. He has served on numerous task forces of the church concerned with agriculture. Now retired in Northfield, Minnesota, he is writing books on agricultural history and rural humor.

Air travelers occupying window seats on a plane winging its way over America's productive Corn Belt can be hypnotized by the squares below, sections and quarter-sections of farmland with their farmsteads scattered evenly over the landscape, clearly defined by shadings of color appropriate to the season.

Those travelers who are of a mechanical turn of mind can calculate the speed of the plane by sighting along the edge of a wing and clocking the mile-squares off with a wristwatch. Those who are of a more philosophical turn may wonder how this remarkable system of food production came into being and how it compares with other systems of the world.

Indeed, if the travelers have flown over many lands in other latitudes, they will be struck by the fact that this checkerboard panorama is seldom seen, even in the better agricultural areas of our earth. They are looking at an aerial view of the family farm system in the United States. If one of them is a business executive or a professional person on his or her way to a convention in a far-off city, chances are quite good that he or she is in fact a product of a family farm, even though being too busy with education and a rise in affluence to give much thought to whence this system of farming and living came and where it may be going.

The family farms which have flourished in America for more than a century and have reached a high level of stewardship and productivity were born of the Homestead Act of 1862. They were nourished by the flow of peasant immigrants who passed under the Statue of Liberty, and sparked by a "Westward ho!" type of entrepreneurship which promised to give every family its own castle on its own land.

There were plenty of selfish motives behind the Homestead Act. The way to establish ownership of territory is to occupy it, the more evenly and thoroughly the better. This was true in preventing encroachment by other nations with colonial intentions, or in crowding out populations which already occupied the land, such as the American Indians or the Spanish of the Southwest. Further, there were new waterways and railroads that sorely needed people and produce to keep them busy and profitable.

Settling new land was in many aspects a ruthless process, as profit-seeking operations often are. But there can be little doubt that spreading family farmers more or less evenly over America contributed to the common good. That is, it served the overall values and purposes of the larger society, in spite of miscalculations and tragic mistakes, such as dividing semiarid lands into plots too small to produce a decent living, and depleting fertility without thought for the future. (After all, until well into this century we thought that to take up fresh land it was necessary only to go farther west.)

Since the author is a product of the Midwest, it is inevitable that this discussion be somewhat tilted toward Corn Belt farming. The fact remains that the American Midwest is still the solid seat of family farming after 120 years, as well as the site of farming's greatest contribution to both American and world food production. Here is where family farms reached their peak of success, not only in land productivity, but in the building of community: schools, churches, rural towns, colleges and universities, cooperatives, local governmental units, and all the institutions of what we like to call "the good life."

Under the homestead system, farmland was divided into relatively small plots, a quarter-section (160 acres) being the most common, with 80 acres often emerging as a normal farm in areas where fertility was good and rainfall ample. These little farms were quickly found to be unrealistic in semiarid regions such as the Dakotas and Montana. The first thing homesteaders had to do was enlarge their holdings. This was a necessity in the Plains and highly desirable even in the best farm country, such as Iowa.

Even so, small family farms were what built rural America as it was known to our grandparents earlier in this century. Looking back on that time with considerable nostalgia, we wonder how the pioneers did it. How could you raise a family on 80 or 160 acres, even send some of the children through college? Our forebears actually lived very well in that horse-and-buggy age, better in some respects than we do now. They created most of the community institutions that we now enjoy and made a good start on the modernization of homes and farm practices.

Labor was cheap, whether you reared your own or hired "newcomers." The small farms were loaded with livestock and all kinds of crops, many of which contributed directly to the feeding of one's family. Farmers, heavily supported by family help, raised their own seed, produced their own fertilizer, and kept cash outlay to a minimum. The small amount of cash generated by the little farms went to pay off land debt, to improve livestock, and to set in motion the mechanization that relieved farm drudgery and paved the way for the labor-efficient but expensive agriculture of today.

Farm Size Increases

Farm enlargement was a means of correcting the miscalculations of the homestead period. It continued steadily through those golden years of the family farm, 1900 to 1920. Around the middle of this period inventive farmers began seriously to replace horses with tractors and to relieve laborious tasks around the farmstead with electric motors.

During this time also the immigration from Europe tapered off. The building of America as an industrial nation was made possible by a steady flow of farm youth pushed off the land by mechanization and educated off the farms by our colleges. Most of them, of course, were drawn off by economic opportunities that were hard to resist.

After a brief slowdown in the early 1930s when depression stagnated cities and industry, the trend toward bigger and heavily mechanized farms took off with a vengeance, until today farmers number less than four percent of our population. For a time we boasted about this great transformation as a triumph of efficiency and excellence. Where else in the world could 1/25th of the people feed all the rest, full measure running over, with extra for export to a hungry world?

American farming has in recent years been the world showcase of science and technology applied to the essential task of feeding growing populations. Agriculture colleges and their extension services warmed to the exciting task of bringing about greater yields and better products. Farmers bought bigger machines and paid high prices for more land to keep the machines busy. The movement of farm-raised people into industry and services accelerated.

As a farm editor I helped this process along at every step and found ways to boast about its success—with only an occasional worry about where the trend would eventually lead us and whether the common good was being served.

The cities choked under the migration from the country and developed suburbanization, which in turn begat a migration of city people onto acreages in the country where they or their parents came from in the first place. As a result, vast amounts of energy are now consumed by commuters living in the country and driving long distances into the city for work.

In recent years there have been sharpened concerns about this trend toward bigger operations, among both farmers themselves and the professionals who were in part responsible and who have basked in the success of modern agriculture's productivity. It has been said that if you find a farmer praying for rain these days

you will find a banker praying right alongside. Whether Republican or Democrat, both farmers and bankers will holler to the government for help when prices fail to sustain the costly system. Most of the flexibility has gone out of farming. There is little opportunity to ride out a crisis, either by a change from a depressed product to something that pays more, or by lying low until things get better.

While we boast about our productivity in bushels and pounds, and point with pride to our labor efficiency as the best in the world, we begin to realize that labor efficiency can be a snare and a delusion. What happens to the labor that is "saved"? This question applies to farmers as well as to the exfarmers who are now expending their labor off the land. Successful farmers still on the land will as likely as not adopt the "corn/soybean/Miami" rotation, while exfarmers spend a lot of time and gas searching for recreation to relieve the monotony of their town work.

Smaller family farms had been more or less labor-intensive. Was the input of family labor, without much thought to hourly compensation, a key to their success? Was there anything particularly wrong with such a system? Will it be necessary to return to more labor-intensive farming if we are to save family farms? Of course, we know that a more moderate-size tractor capable of pulling a three-bottom plow or a four-row planter will require more hours to put in a crop than the $40,000 monster in vogue today. Perhaps it is time to take another look at the hours, who puts them in, and what they really cost.

What *Is* a Family Farm?

Since the term "family farm" has in recent years become more of a battle cry than a unit of measure, it might be well here to give some thought to its definition. Obviously, the unit of farm production that can be handled as a family enterprise has grown rapidly through the years. There are several reasons: the march of mechanization, the adjustment of farming practices to land capability, the curtailment of multiple projects on each farm in favor of greater specialization, the availability of financing, and others.

One workable definition says a family farm is "an agricultural production unit in which the management, economic risk, and most of the labor (peak seasons excepted) are provided by a given family and from which that family receives the bulk of its earnings. Family farms can range from a one-acre tobacco allotment in North Carolina to a Kansas wheat spread of several thousand acres. It is defined not in terms of acreage but of independent entrepreneurship." [1]

Much of our talk is about "the family farm" vs. "the corporation farm." It comes through as a confrontation, but in fact the line between the two is fuzzy. If you think of a corporation as a large company owned by nameless stockholders and operated by salaried management and labor, then corporation farms have not made much headway in America, except in the Southwest and California. In recent years many *family* farms have been legally incorporated for good reasons, such as tax management, limited liability, and better handling of the minority interest of family members who work elsewhere. These are still family farms, but some have acquired characteristics which we think of as belonging to Big Business. Management may be diluted, more of the business is financed on annual borrowings, and the tendency to gobble up neighboring farms gives them an air of ruthlessness.

Along with growth in size, from a $50,000 investment to more like $250,000, such farms acquire substantial handicaps. Among these are the need to hire more labor, buy more land, invest in more machinery, and borrow more money—all making it nearly impossible to keep management within a family or to retain ownership in a family from generation to generation.

The record of larger family farms as food producers, and usually also as stewards of the land, is excellent. Our Corn Belt remains a wonder of the world when it comes to high and sustained yields. Farmers worry more about too much production than too little. This is an amazing phenomenon when one considers the reduction in farm-land through urbanization, the increase in our own population, and the demands of an ever-hungry world which have led to heavy purchase of our agricultural surpluses.

In the early part of this century, the typical farm was not thought of primarily as a production unit for the export of food to cities and to the world. It was the seat of the family, a social and educational unit, a microcosm of human development and, we must not forget, the source of human material for the building of institutions, cities, nations. Its net food production for export was substantial even then, but not its main reason for being.

The difference in net productivity between large modern farms and small family farms has led some concerned people to the conclusion that while the family farm is an attractive institution in theory, we can no longer afford it in view of the growing populations, at home and abroad, who demand the utmost in food production. This well-meaning attitude needs closer scrutiny, however. Larger family farms, utilizing the best agricultural science, are very effective in production and outstrip any kind of big farming found anywhere in the world.

What Are the Alternatives?

The alternatives to family farming are not all that good. The large corporation farms operating in this country, mostly in the West and Southwest, depend heavily on migrant laborers, many of whom are undocumented aliens willing to work at low wages. Labor difficulties are growing for these large farms, costs are soaring, and federally subsidized water is growing scarcer. The tentative growth of corporation farming in the rest of the country has been mostly in the area of canning crops, seed crops, and factory farming of some livestock species. So far the non-family corporations have stayed away from diversified farming.

Farming has not been profitable enough to attract large amounts of capital. I have told my farmer friends for years that the best situation for farming is to have market prices a little on the lean side. This keeps big investment money out and reduces the temptation for family farmers to gobble up more and more land, thereby initiating forces that would kill off the kind of farming which has helped them to prosper.

Corporation farming (and even family farming grown so large that the input of the family is minimal) is going to run into high labor costs, strikes, dropping productivity, and other problems of bigness. There is real doubt whether in the long run these will produce cheap and abundant food. Nor does this new ballgame in American farming show much promise of caring properly for the land or increasing its productivity.

Still another alternative, government-owned and operated farms such as those of the Soviet Union and some other socialist countries, have often turned out to be a disappointment. What better evidence is there than the Soviet practice of allowing their workers to operate a few private acres on their own, these small holdings outstripping the government farms in both efficiency and productivity?

The poor performance of alternate forms of farming has so far been one of the best arguments for preserving our family-farm system. It is time to get serious about dealing with the trends that are threatening this structure of farming.

The common good may well be served best by family-farm units, not only in terms of total food production for domestic and worldwide use, but also through the historic function of farms as social units with important human benefits.

During the last generation we have been more or less committed to the inevitability of large machinery, high energy input, large fields, elimination of fencerows and windbreaks, specialization in crops or livestock, and heavy use of fertilizers and weedkillers. This trend has been based on three premises: (1) substituting technology for human labor is good; (2) economies of scale go on forever; (3) problems of farming can be met indefinitely by increasing research and applied science.

It is amazing what confidence we have had in the idea that we can always meet our problems by pouring on more technology and energy. Low prices are met with higher and higher yields on the theory that it is the extra 10 bushels per acre that make the difference between loss and profit. Instead of holding off on fertilizer when surpluses are piling up, we fertilize at even higher rates. Every threat of insect damage or disease is met with more and better chemicals, which of course add materially to the cash cost of doing business. When insects or diseases develop immunity to our chemicals, we increase the rate of application and urge scientists to come up with new chemicals to keep us ahead of the pests.

This race with disaster becomes more intense with each passing year. The stakes become higher, and dependence on bankers and scientists becomes greater. More farmers —and scientists—are asking, "Can this go on indefinitely?"

Why the Trend Must End

There is almost no flexibility left in large-scale farming. Our vulnerability brings a cry for price supports and government intervention the minute market prices drop. Only conglomerate corporations have the financial reserves to ride out low price periods, and these can get their flexibility from different crops in different parts of the country. They rotate their money instead of their crops.

Individual farmers, trying to go it alone with the help of their local bankers and cooperatives, have lost what was once their greatest strength, diversification. Their debts for machinery and annual outlay for fertilizer and chemicals nearly kill them. Added to the burden is interest on land purchased at unbelievably high rates. They bought their machinery first and then frantically searched for enough land to justify their machinery investment.

There are other traps we have fallen into of late. The resistance of pests to chemicals has been growing markedly. Serious scientists are becoming concerned about their ability to stay ahead in the race. The complicated chemical formulas we have fashioned to fight pests are becoming increasingly suspect because of the environmental damage they may do. The boom is being lowered on our ability to fight off disaster with chemicals.

Fertilizers, which I do not lump with chemicals, have problems of their own. Today our nitrogen comes largely from petroleum or natural gas. Very little of it comes from manure or legumes. This "hydroponics" type of fertilization, in which almost the complete requirements of the crop are placed in the soil before the crop is planted and very little of the plant nutrition is residual in the soil, is very costly and very vulnerable.

The problems of large farm operations in this country certainly point to a revision in our thinking with respect to size and ownership. Unfortunately, there is a growing feeling that farm growth is irreversible because the efficiency of large farms keeps right on improving. But this notion may not be accurate.

For many years I have pleaded for moderation in farm size and operating procedures. The old Aristotelian "golden mean" keeps coming to the fore as a guide to human behavior. I have known hundreds of smart and successful farmers who have taken the middle road in mechanization and size. It was a deliberate decision.

They replaced scoop shovels with power unloading wagons, but they found no really good reason for going all the way into push-button farming.

Moderation in farming looks even better today as we face up to current realities. The substitution of petroleum for labor cannot go on indefinitely. The growing concern over the lavish use of chemicals to stave off agricultural pests is pointing to a return of rotations, which have virtually disappeared from our agricultural scene. The shift back to more forage crops will call for a dispersal of livestock onto smaller farms in the pattern of a generation ago. As time passes and world population grows, we will have to bring into production poorer land, and this will not lend itself to the corn/soybean/Miami rotation but will require the expansion of livestock that can utilize roughages and grazing plants that are high in cellulose.

These changes argue in favor of more traditional family-farm practices, provided of course that family farms can come up with the production efficiency and land and water conservation that we will surely need. The fact is that efficiency and conservation have done rather well under the family-farm system. There is reason to believe that moderate-size farms, family operated, can avail themselves of 80 percent of the efficiency measures open to the very largest farms. The 20 percent shortfall can be made up by the more flexible labor and management characteristics of smaller operations.

What Can Be Done?

If moderate-size family farms are to stage a comeback in this country, there will have to be general acceptance among both farm and non-farm people of certain safeguards. Food production has become too important, both in domestic and international policy, to be left to the decisions of farmers alone! Non-farm people will need to understand farm problems far better than they have in the past in order to make wise decisions related to food production.

Conservation of soil fertility and fresh water supplies is an absolute necessity in the pursuit of the common good. Productive farmland must be protected from urban uses. (Farmers themselves have not always been cooperative and farsighted in matters such as rural zoning and restrictions on use of farmland.)

Since the very essence of family farming is ownership of the land by the operator, there may need to be government restrictions on land purchase, not only by speculators and foreigners but by farmers themselves who grow too greedy in the acquisition of land. Tax structures must favor the keeping of land in farming families. Somehow we have to do away with the single greatest boost to bigness, which is the privilege of avoiding taxes by moving losses around within a large corporate or conglomerate financing structure.

Most of all, we need to tighten up our farm support programs so that the plums do not go heavily toward already-successful large operators. The trouble with government price supports all along has been that if prices are fixed to assure less-efficient operators a decent living, the more efficient grab the ball and run with it in the direction of more land and still bigger operations. Or the government support prices quickly become capitalized in higher land prices, which in themselves become a drag on the family-farm system. Price fixing by government, rather than being the salvation of family farms, can contribute to their destruction. Current proposals in the Congress call for a limit on the total dollar amount any one farm can receive in a year, with declining scales of support as the production increases.

One of the tragedies of our times is that we have become obsessed with the idea of union wages, or at least a minimum wage set by government. Family farms were built on family work and enterprise, with little or no thought to putting a monetary value on each hour of labor. Nor was there much thought among farm people of return on investment. The durability of family farms through the generations has been due mainly to the fact that family labor and ingenuity was poured into the operations without stint. In an urban setting such family input is usually not possible, except in the case of such very small businesses as a ma-and-pa grocery.

It has been pointed out that with rural wives working in town and rural children wrapped up in high school activities there is little or no family labor to be tapped on today's typical farm. Yet it is entirely possible that the trend away from family farms cannot be reversed without the economic advantage of family labor that is increasingly being scattered to the four winds.

There is no use trying to shake off the economic factors in family farming. If the family farm is not a viable economic unit, it will not survive on nostalgia! Farm families need income to supply their needs, just as nonfarm families need income, and that income must be earned by products that can be sold.

At the same time, we need once more to place emphasis on the human factors in family farming. Farms would never have played their important role in the building of community without noneconomic factors such as pride in the care of the land, pride in helping to feed many more people than actually live on the land, satisfaction of family members working and growing together, and many other human values.

The Role of the Church

The arena of values is the sector where the church has a special function in shaping our life and work. The purpose of life and its ultimate meanings—these are the special concern of the church. If every farm family could recognize that its purpose in life is to serve God and care for God's creation, we would avoid most of the excesses that have put U.S. agriculture in trouble.

In its dialog about farming and farmers, the church must set high goals and take pains to recognize the essentials of farm science and good husbandry. It is unfortunate that the church sometimes is tempted to follow the latest fads in farm reform. Usually farmers are the first to recognize church positions that do not square with the realities.

A case in point was a near-miss in the deliberations of the American Lutheran Church at its national convention several years ago. There was great concern over world hunger and the "wastefulness" of U.S. farming. A resolution was offered—and narrowly defeated—urging that American farmers forego the raising of livestock, especially cattle, on the grounds that more people could be fed with fewer acres if all land were used for the direct production of food for people.

The proponents of the resolution completely overlooked two things: the shock that such a shift would administer to the traditional structure of agriculture, with its biologically sound cropping/livestock diversification, and the fact that some animals—ruminants—have the capability of using roughage which cannot be utilized directly by people, thus turning rough feed and grass into the best of food for people such as meat and milk. Also overlooked was the fact that a large percentage of the world's land can and should raise only roughages; it would be destroyed by using it to produce grains and vegetables.

The church has an important role in rebuilding the attitudes of its people to encourage moderate family farming. But the church also has to take an approach marked by intelligence as well as compassion, or it will not be effective in this most important challenge.

For its own sake as an effective institution, as well as for the sake of that large group of church members who do not understand food production, the church needs to weigh and study before it makes pronouncements. It needs to involve farming people at every stage in its development of policy proposals concerning farm and food issues.

Not only must we size up the problems of domestic farming with intelligence and compassion, we need also to be aware of the broad picture of world food needs. That subject is dealt with elsewhere in this book, but I do want to make three points that have a direct bearing on any discussion of family farming:

1. We cannot feed the whole world even though we have some of the world's best land and its most reliable climate for farming. We can only generate modest surpluses to sell to trading partners and to help meet emergencies that will lift the nutrition level in food-deficit countries.[2]

2. The most urgent need is to help people in food-deficient lands to develop their own agricultural resources wisely so that in the future they can come nearer to feeding themselves. Many things about the U.S. family-farm system—widely distributed ownership of land, economic incentives to produce, and a working infrastructure to support food production—can be borrowed and adapted to low-income countries, even though our high-technology *style* of farming is probably not appropriate there.

3. Surging population increases must be brought under reasonable control before it is too late. No kind of farming can feed an unlimited number of people. It would be folly to assume that either family farming or corporation farming can do this. If moderation is to prevail in farming, there must also be moderation in the number of people that will in the future depend on the world's food supply.

Notes

1. Interreligious Task Force on U.S. Food Policy, Washington, D.C., "Family Farming and the Common Good," Hunger No. 7 (February 1977). A more complete discussion of terms appears in Chapter 4.
2. See the discussion of fallacies in Chapter 1.

For Discussion

1. How would you define the "common good"? How many different kinds of people need to benefit from a policy before it can be judged as serving the common good?

2. The author says the trend toward larger and more mechanized farms is based on three premises: (1) substituting technology for human labor is good; (2) economies of scale go on forever; (3) problems of farming can be met indefinitely by increasing research and applied science. Examine the three premises separately and ask whether each is valid. Does the answer vary for the first premise if asked from the viewpoint of the person doing the work or from the viewpoint of society as a whole?

3. What does the author mean in saying, "There is almost no flexibility left in large-scale farming"? Do you agree?

4. How do you react to the statement, "Moderation in farming looks even better today as we face up to current realities"?

5. Should we have government restrictions on land purchase by a single owner? Would such a policy conflict with our concept of private property? Examine these questions in light of the phrase, "the Lord's land." What does that phrase mean to you?

6. "The durability of family farms through the generations has been due mainly to the fact that family labor and ingenuity was poured into the operations without stint." Was that good? Was it oppressive? If you were (or are) a farmer, would it be important for you to earn a dependable and substantial hourly wage? Should the answer for farmers be different from the answer for industrial workers? Why or why not?

7. Reread and discuss each of the last three paragraphs in this chapter.

4

How Can the Smaller
Farm Be Saved?

by Don Reeves*

The land shall not be sold in perpetuity, for the land is mine; for you are strangers and sojourners with me.
Leviticus 25:23

Although most public programs for agriculture are allegedly designed to help family farms, a major conclusion must inevitably be that federal policy on the whole has discouraged small farm operations and, since benefits are usually distributed in direct proportion to volume of output, led to greater concentration in farming.

W. FRED WOODS
Assistant to Deputy Director of Extension
Science and Education Administration
U.S. Department of Agriculture

---

* DON AND BARBARA REEVES are the senior partners (with cousins) in a two-family grain and livestock farm near Central City, Nebraska. Since 1977, Don has spent most of each year in Washington working on farm and food issues with the Friends Committee on National Legislation. He chairs the Agricultural Policy Work Group of the Interreligious Task Force on U.S. Food Policy.

When preparing the Israelite people for nationhood, Moses introduced the concept of sustainable farming, if not by that name. The notion is included in his rules for observing the year of the Sabbath and the year of Jubilee.

Farmers everywhere understand the necessity of being good stewards of the land and the water, if food production is to be sustained. This is my interpretation of the admonition that "in the seventh year there shall be a sabbath of solemn rest for the land" (Lev. 25:4). Unfortunately, our practice does not always measure up to our understanding.

Moses also instructed that certain debts are to be forgiven (Deut. 15:1), those who have slipped into bondage are to be released (Lev. 25:41), and, in the year of Jubilee, each property is to be returned to its original family (Lev. 25:13-16, 23-24).

I interpret these passages, if somewhat freely, as advice that the social institutions which we create, in this instance the structure of agriculture, must not permit too great a concentration of control over the basic resources.

These are instructions with a promise.

Therefore you shall do my statutes, and keep my ordinances and perform them. . . . The land will yield its fruit, and you will eat your fill, and dwell in it securely (Lev. 25:18-19).

What better instructions, and promise, could there be for a system of agriculture based on farm workers having secure tenure on the land—family farms!

The American Family Farm Structure

Until recent decades, at least, the history of agricultural development in the United States has been one of encouragement of dispersed ownership and control of farmland. During the colonial period, particularly in New England, the first order of business in each community was the distribution of land among the families.

Since the time of Jefferson's observation that "small landholders are the most precious part of a state," most federal agriculture policy has been justified in terms of support for family farms. As Americans moved west, the family-farm pattern of New England and Appalachia was extended, specifically by the Northwest Ordinance of 1789. Much of the area west of the Missouri River was settled under the Homestead Act of 1862, which provided 160 acres to virtually any family that would settle and build a home on the acreage and occupy it for at least five years. The family-farm system spread from the north Atlantic coast across the Midwest, the Great Plains, and most of the West and Northwest.

This base has been reinforced by support services, including education, credit, and marketing assistance.

Building on widespread basic public education, the land grant universities, established by the 1862 Morrill Act and its 1890 amendments, formed the core of an extensive training, research, and continuing education program. Other features included the Agricultural Experiment Stations, the Agricultural Extension Services, and vocational agricultural training.

The Federal Farm Loan Act of 1916 and the Farm Credit Act of 1933 laid the way for development of a family of cooperative farm credit institutions.

Marketing assistance can be said to have begun with public chartering of barge canals in the 19th century and includes public subsidies of railroad construction later in that century. Those grants were not without abuse, which led to later regulation of commercial carriers. A landmark of marketing assistance was the Capper-Volstead Act of 1922, which paved the way for an extensive network of farmer-controlled purchasing and marketing cooperatives.

Two exceptions must be noted to the predominant U.S. experience. Across the southern United States the plantation system prevailed. The social and economic effects of slavery and its successor, sharecropping, linger a hundred years after emancipation. There has been differential access to land and community support services, because of both racial and socioeconomic barriers. Basic educational services have lagged; the colleges of 1890 never rivaled their 1862 counterparts. There was not equal access to credit or market facilities.

A second basic exception is in the Southwest, where the first non-Indian settlers were Spanish, and hacienda-type operations became the norm.

Disproportionate rural poverty in much of the southern United States, both as it continues to exist and as it has migrated to urban areas, is almost certainly related to these historically different patterns of agricultural structure. A parallel observation might be made regarding landholding patterns and access to support services, as they relate to rural poverty, in virtually all of the less-developed nations.

Exceptions noted, the U.S. has developed basically a family-farm system of agriculture, and it has been enormously productive. While the agriculture and food system is not without faults, most Americans can enjoy an adequate supply of nutritious food for less of their labor than any other people in all earth's history. In fact, some would maintain that most of us eat too much, to the detriment of both our physical and spiritual health.

Family Farmers: Small, Medium, Large

The title "family farmer" is claimed by a great range of farmers. At one extreme is the person or family living on a plot they *farm* in addition to full-time off-farm employment. The operation provides a rural home and perhaps some supplemental income—although as a class, the cash exchange for these *farms* shows a net loss. The *profit,* if any, lies in the non-money income—produce consumed at home, plus possible savings in housing costs.

Exemplifying the opposite extreme is a California farm operation which involves six households of an extended

Table 2. Farms by Value of Sales, 1976
(using 1959 USDA definition of "farm")

	up to $20,000	$20-40,000	$40-100,000	$100,000 and up	all farms
Number of farms	1,996,000	320,000	307,000	155,000	2,778,000
% of total farms	71.9%	11.5%	11.0%	5.6%	100%
% of total cash receipts (derived)	10.0%	10.1%	20.3%	59.6%	100%
Cash receipts from farming, incl. other income, per farm	$ 4,825	$30,453	$63,753	$370,807	$34,704
Non-money farm income, per farm	$ 2,350	$ 2,644	$ 3,212	$ 4,490	$ 2,599
Realized gross income, per farm	$ 7,175	$33,097	$66,965	$375,297	$37,303
Production expenses, per farm	$ 4,616	$23,472	$50,407	$319,581	$29,418
Realized net income, per farm	$ 2,559	$ 9,622	$16,558	$ 55,716	$ 7,885
Realized net as % of realized gross income, per farm	35.6%	29.0%	24.7%	14.8%	21.1%
Off-farm income, per farm	$12,533	$ 5,762	$ 6,906	$ 13,310	$11,174
Total income, per farm	$15,092	$15,384	$23,464	$ 69,026	$19,059

Source: U.S. Dept. of Agriculture, Economic Research Service Bulletin #576

family, 38 other full-time employees plus 125 seasonal workers, and gross farm sales of several million dollars per year. They also think of themselves as a family farm operation.

My own definition of a "family farm" is an agricultural production unit in which the members of a family assume the risk and provide the management and the majority of the labor, peak seasons excepted. I would call it a "small family farm" if it might be expected to produce, at most, a minimum living for an operating family. With variations by commodity, this would include nearly all farms having gross sales of less than $40,000 per year and certainly all those having less than $20,000 per year. By this definition, at least 2 million of the 2.6 million farmers in the country are small farmers.

When I speak of a "large farm," I refer to those larger than necessary to achieve most efficiencies of scale of production and having at least partial separation of management, risk, and labor, even within closely related families. This would include all of those 10,000 farms having gross sales of $500,000 or more and most of the 40,000 farms having sales between $200,000 and $500,000.

"Moderate-size farms," then, are those left in the middle—between 1/3 and 1/2 million farms on which the managing family does the work and has some expectation of a reasonable income from farming (or ought to!).

Cyrus McCormack, John Deere, Henry Ford, Rudolph Diesel

Superimposed on our family-farm structure has been the whole process of industrialization. Sparked by a series of inventions ranging from the steel plowshare to the internal-combustion engine and solid-state electronics, fed by relatively low-priced fossil fuels, and fanned by relatively high labor-income expectations, the process has made several million farm families superfluous.

No matter what date you count as beginning this process, it has reached full flower since World War II. Nearly two-thirds of the almost 7 million U.S. farms of the 1930s have disappeared, many to urban, suburban, and industrial development, but the large majority to consolidation.[1]

This rapid consolidation is being increasingly regarded as a mixed blessing. The availability of ample, relatively low-cost food has been noted and emphasized. But there is growing concern that the consolidation is moving both further and faster than is necessary or, more importantly, than may be possible without threatening our basic agricultural structure and the well-being of farm families and rural communities. Not less than eight U.S. religious denominations have approved formal statements of concern during recent years.[2]

How then are we to decide whether continued farm consolidation, or new patterns of ownership and management, should be accepted, endorsed, or opposed? What are the criteria by which the Christian community might judge?

It has been my privilege, during the past 30 months, to be in nearly 50 gatherings where there was open sharing on the theme, "What spiritual values attend a family-farm system of agriculture?" Many of the groups considered a related question, "Do these values relate to size of farm in any consistent manner?"

Several persistent themes have emerged during these times of sharing:

1. Responsibility for the nurture of growth, both plant and animal, renews kinship with God's creation and acknowledges our role in the created world.

2. Sharing of work assignments and decision making can be an important part of family life and child-rearing.

3. The attitudes of sharing and caring developed in joint family ventures carry over into community life.

4. Self-reliance is fostered by independent entrepreneurs.

5. Individuals and families benefit from having a large measure of control over their own life and work situations.

6. Workers need to be able to identify with the product of their labor; reducing labor to nothing more than a commodity is somehow "alienating."

7. The highest level of stewardship of natural resources depends on an intimacy that is probably more difficult in large-scale operations and may be absent if farmland is only an investment.

8. There is a correlation between the number and variety of business and social institutions in a rural community and the number of farm owners in the surrounding area.

9. There is almost certainly a greater sharing of community decision making in communities surrounded by small and moderate-size farms.

10. In most groups, there was an expression, but not always consensus, that somehow "small" is better than "large." When expressed, there was usually consensus that largeness *per se* is not a positive value.

What About Efficiency?

Family farms are generally regarded as being at least as—if not more—efficient than larger hired-labor operations, in part because of owner-operator willingness to give more of themselves. Family farmers usually feel they are more innovative (often from necessity) than employees, particularly those on larger industrialized farms.

Clearly, widespread use of equipment, together with biological and chemical changes, has reduced the labor and overall economic costs of raising foodstuffs. A few specialty crops will continue to require hand labor. As energy costs continue to escalate, there may be some modifications in the kinds of equipment or techniques used. For the most part, however, American expectations

of wages are so high that labor will not be substituted for machinery to any great extent in the foreseeable future, especially if only economic costs are considered.

Our normal accounting of efficiency—i.e., on-farm cost per unit of production, or units of production per hour of labor—is seriously deficient in ways that ought to concern Christians. There is a bundle of what we might call social and community costs, which have had little notice or discussion in public policy considerations and which, taken as a whole, increase as farms are consolidated and the number of farming opportunities decreases.

Some of these are *economic* costs, which may be estimated if not precisely measured; for example: costs of moving and retraining farm families who leave farms; some portion of welfare and social service costs for families who do not find alternative employment; increasing costs of community services for declining populations; and costs of training young people who then have no farm or other job opportunity to keep them in the community.

Other social and community costs are less tangible, and correspond with the *spiritual* values listed above. It may be impossible to assign monetary value to these, even if there is general agreement that they are real and are an important factor in considering what sort of farming structure we wish to create or maintain.

Combining social and community costs with economic costs would suggest an optimum size of farm (B-C in Figure 1) smaller than the optimum size defined only by traditional measures of efficiency. There will be a continuing dialog over the trade-offs (A-B, C-D). The economic cost of depending on a large number of very small farms (smaller than A) for our total food supply would doubtless be unacceptable, yet it would seem inappropriate to place barriers in the way of families who choose such operations. We might even choose to deliberately encourage or modestly subsidize such farms under some circumstances. On the other hand, there would seem to be little justification for public policies which encourage or subsidize growth in individual farms beyond the size at which most economies of scale can be achieved (larger than D). For most commodities, this point is reached on moderate-size farms, as I have defined them.

Present farm programs and policies, including tax policies, seem to have the effect of encouraging and even subsidizing the current trend toward continued consolidation, probably in unintended ways.

Figure 1. Economic and Social Costs of Farm Commodities Related to Size of Farm Production Unit

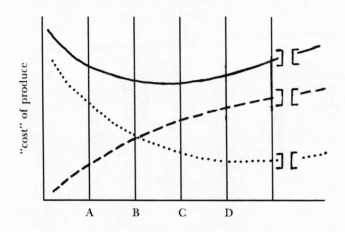

size of farm production unit

. . . . per unit (economic) cost of production

- - - - social and community "costs" of increasing farm size

—— total "costs" of production

What follows here is a brief review of several specific policy issues which are, or probably should be, under continuing review as they influence the kind of farms we encourage or discourage.

Commodity Prices—Farmers' Income

Farm family incomes have fallen short of non-farm family incomes nearly every year since the early 1950s and during many earlier times. Farmers have been squeezed between rapidly accelerating farm costs and fluctuating but usually lagging increases in farm prices.

In recognition of the inability of individual farm producers to influence farm commodity prices, and the basic importance of the food-producing sector, there have been federal farm price support programs since 1933. Because these programs have generally focused on commodity prices—price per bushel or per bale—benefits have gone to farmers in proportion to their quantity of production. Larger farmers have benefited more than small or moderate-size farmers.

In 1978, for example, nearly 50% of the program payments went to the largest 10% of the participating farmers (average, $10,900 per farm), while the smallest 50% of the farms shared only 10% of the payments ($460 per farm). Increases in 1978 market prices (estimated to range from 3% for cotton to 14% for wheat) benefited all producers, but again in proportion to production.

There have been dollar payment limitations in several programs, but they have been so high as to have little impact. In 1978, for example, only 1184 (0.2%) of the participants were affected by a $40,000 limit ($52,500 for rice).[3]

There is a strong tendency among farmers to use any money left over after basic living expenses to expand their farm operation. The availability of substantial program payments has thus further increased the advantage of large farmers over small and moderate-size farmers as competitors for available farmland. This is clearly demonstrated by recent transfers of farmland—65% to 75% of farm purchases during recent years have been for farm enlargement.

Commodity programs, as they have operated, have almost surely accelerated the trend toward fewer, larger farms. Several suggestions have been made for changes which might temper or reverse this effect: reducing the dollar payment limit, or limiting eligibility for commodity program support to a moderate quantity of production; supporting the price on the first block of each farmer's produce at a higher level, perhaps with several steps down to low, or no, support beyond a moderate quantity; limiting eligibility to producers who depend on farm income for a substantial share of the family income, or excluding producers who have large non-farm incomes, especially non-farm corporate producers. Similar limitations have been suggested for federal crop insurance programs.

Income payments unrelated to production have been mentioned for small producers, but these probably fit better into some overall welfare or income assurance program.

Changes in commodity programs will require both a clearer definition of desired farm structure and probable effect of a range of programs than presently exists.

World Trade and Grain Reserves

United States grain exports have expanded rapidly since 1970 and show every sign of continuing to grow. More than one-third of our farmland is now used to supply more than one half of all grain in international trade. So, U.S. commodity pricing policies, although focused on producer incomes, have a major impact worldwide. The U.S. support price becomes the floor for the world price.

Prices set too low may seem attractive to American consumers, but also mean that we export our grain too cheaply, and grain is the principal commodity available in exchange for imports, notably oil. Prices too high may have a very adverse effect in the developing nations who now take one-third of our grain exports. But prices too low may be a disincentive for poor nations to take the difficult steps to increase their own food production.

Weather variability and political decisions resulting in unexpected demand for grain suggest the need for a substantial grain reserve. Such a reserve should be a joint international venture, but in its absence, the U.S. should not wait. In 1977 Congress established a program under which farmers contract to hold their own grain for up to three years, within a certain price range. Its first full year of operation indicated that it is possible to withdraw grain from the market and bolster prices during a time of ample supply, then release it during a time of shorter supply. The debate continues as to what is the most equitable range of prices for accumulation and release. Since these become the effective floor and ceiling for grain prices, farmers feel very strongly that they must be equitable.

As of this writing, Congress still needs to establish a smaller grain reserve, probably mostly wheat, to be held very tightly by the federal government and used only to help guarantee continuity in the Food for Peace program.

Income Tax Rules

Federal tax rules, as applied to farmers, provide incentives for expansion and concentration. Many business tax rules also apply to farmers. In addition, special tax rules were created and justified for farmers as small business operators with peculiar needs. However, the benefits flow primarily to taxpayers in high income brackets who report income from farming, whether their principal income is from farm or non-farm sources. Well-established farmers benefit more than small farmers since most of the tax savings are proportional to the marginal income tax bracket.

The tax rules which help farmers level income from good to poor years also encourage non-farm investors to enter farming to create artificial "losses" which can be counted against their non-farm income for tax purposes.

These rules cost the public treasury nearly $1 billion each year and create severe competition, particularly for small and moderate-size farmers who earn their living from farming. These farmers would probably be better off if the special farm tax rule were eliminated altogether. Another approach might be to limit eligibility, on the basis either of total income or of income from non-farm sources.

Preferred tax treatment of capital gains promotes investment in farmland on the basis of speculation rather than productivity, driving land prices even higher. Making future gains in farmland value ineligible for capital gains treatment might slow such increase, to the relative advantage of small or beginning farmers.

Access to Land—Succession

Large capital investment, high labor income expectations, inflation, the operation of commodity programs, the effect of income tax rules—it is no wonder that less than half the farmers who retire are being replaced by young farmers! Yet if we are serious about a sustainable, dispersed agricultural structure, we must enable younger families to become established in farming.

In addition to the previous suggestions, which are mostly in the nature of reducing competition, mention should be made of more positive types of direct assistance. More generous terms for credit for beginning farmers is often mentioned, and a few modest programs are in place, primarily through the Farmers Home Administration. Church bodies owning farmland and other farmowners who are not operators might consider younger families as preferred tenants. At least one state has an outright land purchase/restricted-lease program in place for young farmers. A few very bold groups continue to experiment with land trusts or other devices by which a community-based group can assure security of tenure without the expectation that each farm generation pay for the land again.

As farm estates have increased in value, inheritance taxes are seen as a barrier to passing family farms from one generation to the next, particularly for families who do not make any advance plans. Changes made in the 1976 tax law, combined with wills and other permissible planning tools, now make possible the passing of moderate-size farms ($400,000 to $500,000) without serious tax consequences, if non-farming heirs do not wish to cash out their equity. It is debatable how much beyond that it is advisable to go.

There is some fear that other features of the 1976 law—use valuation and extended tax payments—may give an extraordinary benefit to certain larger farm estates and move us in the direction of a "landed class." At least it may be observed that too great advantage to some classes of landowners—corporate, institutional, or by inheritance—will require that we give more assistance to beginning farmers. Help to young farmers might well include assistance to potential *heirs* of farm property.

New Patterns in Farming Communities

It seems unlikely that tomorrow's farming communities will be like those of either today or yesterday.

Continuation of present trends will lead to fewer, larger farms. An increasing number of these, on a commodity-by-commodity basis, will become integrated with processors or suppliers or both. Present tax laws, both income and inheritance, will make incorporation and, in some instances, later takeover by larger corporations attractive. It seems likely that the family character of many of these operations will disappear, and so also will many rural communities as we have known them.

Moderate-size farms seem the hardest-squeezed by present circumstances. It would seem possible to make these more viable with rather modest changes in present public policies, enabling the continuation of thriving rural communities.

It is my expectation that we will see a continuing large number of small farms, part-time farms, and rural residences, on which families live and earn part of their livelihood. For some, this will be a stepping stone to a full-time farm operation; for others, it will be a permanent arrangement. On such farms families should be able to achieve a very high quality of family and community life.

Among the small-farm families are some who deliberately choose to free themselves of bondage to the materialistic world most of us are caught up in and devote themselves to establishing new patterns of living, to finding new (or old, or eternal) ways of measuring achievement. From their lives and experiments may come a body of values and experience which will serve us all well—perhaps in the almost foreseeable future. We should encourage such ventures.

The United States has not seriously included small and part-time units in farm policy considerations. It is time that we do so.

Finally, be reminded that as sojourners in the land, we are accountable both to our Lord and to our grandchildren. Thinking of our use of the physical resources of land and water and air, and of the nature of the social institutions we create and maintain, are they sustainable? Can we leave both our physical and our social environment better than we found them?

Notes

1. The 1979 Census of Agriculture actually calculates about 2.3 million farms, using the "new" definition of $1000 or more sales, or about 2.6 million using the "old" definition of $250 or more sales or 10 acres plus at least $50 sales.

2. See the following statements:

   "Economic Problems of Rural America," Office of Research and Analysis, The American Lutheran Church, 422 South 5th St., Minneapolis, Minn. 55415, 1970, single copy free.

   "The Church and Farm Issues," from *This Land: Ours for a Season,* Church of the Brethren, 110 Maryland Ave., NE, Washington, D.C. 20002, 1974.

   "Agriculture," from *Statement of Legislative Policy,* Friends Committee on National Legislation, 245 Second St., NE, Washington, D.C. 20002, 1977.

   "Ethical Goals for Agricultural Policy," General Board, National Council of Churches of Christ in the USA, 475 Riverside Drive, New York, N.Y. 10027, 1958.

   "Rural America: Life and Issues," Office of Church in Society, United Church of Christ, 475 Riverside Drive, New York, N.Y. 10027, 1979.

   "Agricultural and Rural Life Issues," Board of Church and Society, The United Methodist Church, 100 Maryland Ave., NE, Washington, D.C. 20002, 1976.

   "Who Will Farm?" Church and Society Program Area, United Presbyterian Church in the USA, 1244 Interchurch Center, 475 Riverside Drive, New York N.Y. 10027, 1978.

   "Protecting the Family Farm," Committee on Social Development and World Peace, United States Catholic Conference, 1312 Massachusetts Ave., NW, Washington, D.C. 20005, 1979.

3. U.S. Department of Agriculture, Economics, Statistics, and Cooperative Service, "Status of the Family Farm: Second Annual Report to the Congress," Agricultural Economic Report No. 434 (September 1979).

For Discussion

1. Reflect on Lev. 25:18-19. How do you interpret these instructions and this promise?

2. Do you think the definition of a family farm is a fair and workable one?

3. Review the "persistent themes" listed on pages 65-66. Do they fit the question about spiritual values related to family farming? How do the themes relate to the question of *size*, in your opinion?

4. List five or six social and community *costs*. Can you make a similar list of social and community *benefits?*

5. Should commodity price support programs be changed so that they have a different impact on farm structure? What should be the goals of such programs?

6. Review the section "Fallacy 1" on pp. 14-17 of Chapter 1 and compare that information with the section on World Trade and Grain Reserves in this chapter. What should be the response of the U.S. to efforts to create an international emergency grain reserve?

7. For grain farmers and other experts only: Do you believe the farmer-held domestic grain reserve is working well for farmers? For hungry people? Do you think it should be changed? If so, how? What would be the effect of your proposed changes on farmers? On hungry people?

8. If you own or operate a small non-farm business, do any of the tax problems mentioned in this chapter seem similar to what you experience as a non-farm small business person?

9. One of the states which has an outright land purchase/restricted-lease program in place is Minnesota. Texas has recently passed similar legislation. Have there been bills on the subject introduced in your state legislature in the past decade? Do you think such legislation is a good idea? Would it be useful to invite your legislator to discuss the idea with a group in your congregation?

5

The Land: Who Shall Control?

by Stephen E. Bossi*

While the farmer holds the title to the land, actually it belongs to all the people because civilization itself rests upon the soil. Those who labor in the earth are the chosen people of God. THOMAS JEFFERSON

* STEPHEN E. BOSSI is a research consultant on natural resources, food and farm policy, based in Seattle. He is a former staff member of the National Catholic Rural Life Conference, with offices in Des Moines.

The nature and productivity of agriculture through-out human history have been determined by two key factors: the quality of the land itself and the relationship between the land and the people dependent on it.

The quality of America's land varies widely but our nation includes some of the richest soils in the world. Our climate and topography and the availability of abundant water, coupled with our rich and deep topsoils, constitute an incredibly bountiful food producing resource.

The relationship between the people of America and that resource is not easy to characterize. The patterns of ownership and use of our land are products of many factors, some rooted in the traditional values of our people, some based on recent experience and the demands of the times. However, just because those current patterns evolved over time does not mean they are necessarily the best in terms of the needs of the present or the future. Determining what would be best requires a look back as well as a look ahead. This chapter proposes to do both.

If one had to pick a point in time when the relationship between the land and the people of America received clearest definition, one would probably choose the 15 years between 1774 and 1789. This period, from the adoption of the Declaration on Violation of Rights by the First Continental Congress to the approval of the final language of the Bill of Rights to the U.S. Constitution, was a period of examination of tradition, values, and current experiences. The authors of the founding documents of our country written during this period knew they were engaged in an historic exercise. So they drew upon the knowledge and attitudes of their own times to frame principles that would stand the test of history.

The resources upon which they drew were the same as those we would have to use in a similar effort today. Being a religious people, they looked at the biblical and faith tradition handed down to them. Many of the writers were well educated and thus were also conscious of the philosophical ideas developed throughout western civilization and being actively debated in Europe during the 18th century. Finally, these were people who had firsthand knowledge of the weaknesses of European and colonial land tenure systems. They saw clearly the need to explore *new* approaches in what was to them a new and almost limitless land.

The Faith and the Land

The faith tradition of the American people stretches all the way back to the first book of the Hebrew Bible. The book of Genesis, in its earliest chapters, establishes three basic principles with regard to the land:

- *that the earth belongs to God;*
- *that it is good;*
- *that humans are to "cultivate and care for" it.*

These principles are repeated throughout the Old Testament. In the book of Leviticus God says, "Land must not be sold in perpetuity, for the land belongs to me, and to me you are only strangers and guests" (25: 23 JB). The Psalms repeat, "To Yahweh belong earth and all it holds, the world and all who live in it" (24: 1 JB).

An additional theme of the Hebrew Scriptures is that the earth is to provide for the needs of all. Leviticus describes the year of Jubilee as the opportunity for all debts to be resolved and for each person to have access to the land. It calls for some of the harvest to be left in the field "for the poor and the stranger" (23:22 JB). In Deuteronomy the Lord tells the Israelites to leave some food "for the stranger, the orphan and the widow" (24: 19 JB).

In the New Testament these principles are reaffirmed. "The earth and everything that is in it belong to the Lord" (1 Cor. 10:27 JB). "Everything God has created is good" (1 Tim. 4:4 JB). "If you cannot be trusted with what is not yours, who will give you what is your very own?" (Luke 16:12 JB). The Christian tradition also carries a strong message to give up the personal possession of material goods and distribute them to the poor (Matt. 19:21), or to use them for the good of the community (Acts 4:32).

These scriptural teachings and the ways they were put into practice by the early Christian community started a debate over land policy that has continued throughout subsequent history. Scripture seems to be saying two things:

1. If the earth belongs to God, and if human beings are mandated to share what they have with one another, then it would seem that the created world is not to be controlled by individuals for their own private purposes but is the common heritage of all and should be owned and managed in common.

2. On the other hand, in order to steward the land and to provide for each family, individuals *must* be assigned specific responsibility for defined areas. In other words, some form of *private* ownership seems to be essential if the *common* good is to be served.

In parts of the Old Testament, the rights of private ownership are strongly affirmed. In transmitting God's law to the people of Israel, Moses includes "a curse on him who displaces his neighbour's boundary mark" (Deut. 27:17 JB). This crime is cited many times in the Hebrew Bible (Job 24:2; Hosea 5:10), suggesting the seriousness of taking away an individual's land, the source of one's livelihood. Similarly, Isaiah warns, "Woe to those who add house to house and join field to field until everywhere belongs to them and they are the sole inhabitants of the land" (5:8 JB).

The theme of common ownership and the common purpose of created things appears in the Gospels, particularly in Luke, and is expressly stated in the Acts of the Apostles. But it was the early Christian communities that most clearly defended this practice. One of the leading teachers of this era, St. John Chrysostom, wrote that common ownership was more "in accordance with nature" than private ownership. Another fourth-century teacher, Ambrose of Milan, argued that common property originated in nature and that private property was the result of "immoral usurpation."

Even among the writers of Roman law, there was a difference of opinion over whether private property was an institution of nature or of human laws. This philosophical argument continued for several hundred years, a period during which *church* ownership of land was growing and a German tradition which put limits on the rights of private owners was evolving as an alternative to the absolute freedom of land ownership under Roman law.

By the time of the Reformation, the accepted view of property held that private ownership is necessary for the organization of society but that ownership must be regulated by the state in order to protect the public good. The extent of that regulation, particularly regarding opportunities for individuals to own land, became one of the major causes of the breakdown of monarchies in Europe and the movement of many settlers to North America. The philosophical problem was simply whether the state had the power to restrict the accumulation of property and wealth in order to assure a more equal distribution.

By the end of the 17th century, Europe had undergone several major struggles over land. The era of feudalism had provided an experience of the dependency associated with not having control over the land. During the enclosure movement in England, when peasants were driven off the land to become an exploited industrial labor force, working people learned that *land*lessness can mean *power*lessness. The emergence of landowning yeoman farmers demonstrated that the ownership of even a small parcel of land can be a source of security and independence.

A Little Land for Everyone

These lessons were not lost on the colonial settlers of the United States. Even though the patterns of colonial settlement varied widely, from small townships in New England to large plantations in the South, the concept of "fee simple" ownership was almost universal in the 13 colonies by the mid-18th century. The right to own a piece of land was so widely accepted that it was listed as a fundamental human right in many of the documents of the time.

The Declaration on Violation of Rights, adopted by the First Continental Congress in 1774, specified that the inhabitants of British Colonies "are entitled to life, liberty and property." The Virginia Bill of Rights, adopted in June of 1776, included among the "inherent rights" of all persons "the means of acquiring and possessing property." By using such language as "inherent rights," the founders of this nation sought to justify their demands for protection of private property against the whims of a king or government.

Thomas Jefferson, however, questioned whether the right to property was "inherent" or "natural." He would not put it in the same category as life and liberty because he felt that in order to protect the well-being of society the state may have to tax or even condemn a person's property. It was thus Jefferson's hand that, in framing the Declaration of Independence, substituted "the pursuit of happiness" for "property" in its formulation of the "unalienable rights" of humans. Property, Jefferson seemed to be saying, is a means to an end and not an end in itself.

As a keen student of European history and contemporary philosophy, Jefferson also insisted that one responsibility of government is to make land available to the citizenry. In a frequently-quoted letter sent to James Madison in 1785 he said, ". . . it is not too soon to provide by every possible means that as few as possible shall be without a little portion of land. The small landholders are the most precious part of a state. . . ." It was this defense of widespread distribution of land ownership that Jefferson had argued as chairman of a committee set up in 1784 to decide how the public domain acquired by the new government in the Revolutionary War would be used.

Jefferson felt that the public domain should be given away free to individual settlers. In the Land Ordinance of 1785, however, Congress decided to use its new lands as a source of revenue (in part to pay off war debts), and so set a price of $1 per acre on 640-acre parcels as the minimum purchase. The price was beyond the reach of most people, so less money than expected was raised. Many people, acting on their belief that they were entitled to a piece of land, simply chose to settle as squatters.

A final piece of the framing of U.S. land policy during this period occurred when Congress approved the text of the Bill of Rights in 1789. Jefferson was an early advocate of the need for a Bill of Rights in our Constitution and supported the purpose of the Fifth Amendment, which grants protection to property owners. That Amendment, the basis for numerous court decisions regarding the rights of property owners, provides that the government cannot condemn an individual's land without following proper procedures, "due process of law," and paying "just compensation."

Our Experience Settling the Land

These religious, philosophical, and legal foundations of America's land policies explain only part of the newly-emerging relationship between the land and the people of the land. The rest is found in the experience of the people in settling it. The land was, by European standards, virgin territory. The Indians had not developed a society based on land settlement familiar to the European immigrants. Thus the colonizers viewed the land as vacant and available for "development" in the European sense.

There was, indeed, a sense of conquering the wilderness, of opening up "new" lands. The native people's attitudes of living in harmony with nature, leaving the land undivided as a common heritage, and defining community life in terms of the migration of animals and the phases of nature—these were largely foreign to the colonial frame of mind. In fact, even the process of releasing grants of land for settlement could not move fast enough to satisfy the drive to conquer this "wilderness." Long before independence there were squatters in large numbers populating the frontier areas to the west. It was this spirit of *claiming* the land that Robert Frost captured in his famous line, "The land was ours before we were the land's."

The settlers experienced a further sense that the land of this new world was almost limitless. Many of them must have shared the awe of the Frenchman, Alexis de Toqueville, who wrote of his American travels in 1831:

> The most extraordinary thing of all is the land. . . . There are still, as on the first days of creation, rivers whose founts never run dry, green and watery solitudes, and limitless fields never yet turned by the plowshare.[1]

This sense of limitless wilderness had two effects on the attitudes of the colonial settlers. It allowed them, first, to exploit the land with no concern for the future. Soil erosion or the depletion of nutrients, particularly in the tobacco and cotton regions, were not seen as problems because one could simply move on and clear new land. Second, it persuaded them that the land should be cheap. In fact, some of the wealthy families attempted to establish feudal systems on their estates and found that immigrants would not work for a landlord when they could easily acquire land of their own.

These two attitudes, that land could be exploited because there's always more and that it should be easy to buy, were major factors in U.S. land policy from the time of Independence onward. Some additional values were shaped by the experience of obtaining a piece of land, carving out a homestead, and surviving in the wilderness: the values of independence, individualism, self-confidence, and freedom. They were identified by a great 19th-century historian of the frontier, Frederick Jackson Turner, who argued that by instilling these values in waves of settlers throughout our first 150 years of history, the frontier was an effective promoter of democracy.

Almost as a warning, Turner described it as a democracy "born" of free land, strong in selfishness and individualism, intolerant of administrative experience and education, and pressing individual liberty beyond its proper bounds." [2] Thus, the combination of traditional religious and philosophical attitudes with the experience of settling an untamed and "free" land had created an atmosphere of "diversity and conflict" in which freedom would be exercised in a continuing national debate over land policies.

Jefferson's negotiation of the huge Louisiana Purchase in 1803 fed the thirst for land and responded to the Jeffersonian principle that every citizen should have the opportunity to own a piece of land. Throughout the first half of the 19th century, the Congress passed a series of Public Land Acts which reduced the price on public lands from a $2 per acre level (set in 1796) to $1.25 and reduced the minimum purchase unit from 640 to 80 acres. The Preemption Act of 1841 gave squatters rights to land they had settled and developed—up to 160 acres at a price of $1.25 per acre.

Homestead, Reclamation, and Extension

All of these moves responded to continual public pressure, fueled by advocates such as Horace Greeley of the *New York Tribune* ("Go West, young man . . ."). The pressure was simply that public land be made available to settlers *for free*. In 1862, Congress finally passed the Homestead Act, granting 160 acres to settlers on vacant land who made improvements in that land over a five-year period. While subject to abuse and fraud by speculators, the Homestead Act opened the floodgates to settlement of the Midwest and West.

By 1890, nearly one million entries had been filed for homestead land. Most of them were from families intending to establish themselves on the land. In the words of historian Paul Wallace Gates, "The Homestead Act was the farmers' act. It contributed mightily to drawing population to the frontier, to making family farm ownership easier, and somewhat to reducing dependence on borrowed capital." [3]

The Homestead Act was a turning point in U.S. farm policy, shifting the use of public lands from serving as a government revenue source to promoting a dispersed pattern of land settlement. In the 1902 congressional debate over enactment of the Reclamation Act, Senator Clark of Wyoming cited the Homestead Act as "a means of building up sturdy law-abiding communities of patriotic citizens who, having local habitation and a home, shall constitute an unlimited bank account of patriotism upon which the nation can confidently rely and draw in times of national distress and peril."

This rationale for using government policy to encourage settlement was heard again and again in Congress as subsequent farm and land legislation was proposed and debated. The Reclamation Act of 1902 specifically limited the size and type of farm unit eligible to receive federally-subsidized irrigation water. The Smith-Lever Act of 1914, creating the Cooperative Extension Service, aimed at making agricultural information available to family farmers right in their communities.

By the beginning of this century, the U.S. was firmly committed to a family-farm system of agriculture. The number of farms had grown from about 1.5 million in 1850 to 5.7 million in 1900, peaking eventually at about 6.8 million in 1935. (There were under 2.7 million as of 1979.) A powerful farm bloc in Congress served this large farm community by authoring bills to meet the credit, research, and marketing needs of farmers.

During the 1920s and 1930s, major concern focused on alleviating the price-depressing effects of surplus production. The Agricultural Adjustment Act of 1933 initiated certain controls on crops and marketing. The Farm Credit Act passed that same year sought to speed farm modernization by making credit available for purchase of new equipment and supplies. After 1935 the number of farms began to decline while the average farm size increased rapidly. Between 1940 and 1970 the number of farms was reduced by almost half, while farm size nearly doubled. By 1976, the largest 5.6% of our farms were producing 59.6% of our farm output.

Questions About Farming's Future Shape

America's farm structure today is largely the product of economic and political forces that have been at work at least since the 1930s. Through the land-grant university system and its research stations, new farm techniques relying on mechanization, hybrid seeds, fertilizers, pesticides, and herbicides have been developed. Farm credit programs, tax incentives, and extension efforts have made these techniques known and accessible to farmers. Moreover, the closing of the frontier—the end of the homestead lands—caused the value of farmland to rise, making it more attractive to speculators but also adding to its equity value for financing farm expansion and mechanization.

These forces are still at work. They effectively define the type of agriculture with which our nation will enter the next century. As the number of families left on the land has declined and as the amount of investment in agriculture by non-farm interests has grown, the public has begun to question the direction of existing policies. The food crisis of the early 1970s and a complex legal battle over enforcement of the Reclamation Act's public water provisions have contributed to a questioning of the type of agriculture this country should be encouraging.

That questioning focuses mainly on whether larger scale units, with their greater dependence on capital, fossil-fuel energy, and high technologies, are more dependable and desirable than smaller, more labor-intensive farming units. The questioning amounts to a testing of each of these types of agriculture against the experience of 200 years of land policy in America and against the values which motivate our society and our public decision making.

One area of that testing involves the values espoused by Jefferson: using the land to promote equality and the protection of individual rights. Those values demand widespread access to land ownership and a large degree of freedom in the use of that land. One of the major controversies in agriculture today involves the high cost of land and the fact that price restricts access to ownership. During the four-year period between 1975 and 1979, farm land prices increased by 64.2 percent—much faster than general inflation—to a national average of $560 per acre, with the best land selling for over $2000 an acre. Thus, just the land cost of a moderate-size farm runs between $250,000 and $500,000. Obviously, new farmland ownership is restricted to those having large capital or credit capabilities.

But land prices are not the only restraint on ownership. Farm income statistics developed by the U.S. Department of Agriculture reveal that farming is, at best,

a financially insecure way of life. In the five-year period 1973 to 1977, the rise in farm income did not nearly keep pace with the rise in farm production costs. Net income per farm fell by nearly 39 percent to a near-poverty level of $7200. Those who cannot supplement their income from non-farm work or survive long periods of low income, even net losses, are effectively excluded from U.S. agriculture.

Competition for land, however, comes largely from three sources: (1) present farmers seeking to enlarge their operations to take advantage of new technologies; (2) public and private interests demanding land for non-farm purposes such as urban residential and commercial development, power plants, water reservoirs, parks, and highways; and (3) investment interests speculating in the rising value of farmland or diversifying their investments to include agriculture. All of these tend to come into the land market better financed than the individual wanting to start farming. The fact that the number of farms in the U.S. continues to decline by about 40,000 per year, and that black-owned land is rapidly disappearing, suggests that opportunities for farmland ownership are not as widely or as equitably dispersed as they once were.

What Is "Efficient Farming"?

A second area of testing the advantages of large-scale agriculture against the traditional family-size operation is based on the religious and philosophical principle that property is intended to serve the well-being of all. The concept of the *common good,* when applied to farmland, would demand that land be used in such a way that the basic human needs of all are being met. These needs are for more than just having enough food, fiber, and shelter, though they certainly begin there. They include having a job from which one earns the purchasing power to obtain with dignity the food, shelter, clothing and other goods necessary for life. They also include such things as a livable environment and a sense of security about the future.

Whatever else one might say, American agriculture has certainly been successful in providing abundant food. Throughout the middle half of this century, when farm size has increased as the number of farms decreased, food surpluses have been our major farm problem far more often than food shortages. In fact, those food surpluses, with their resulting low prices, have been a major factor in driving many farmers into bankruptcy and out of farming. During periods of high unemployment in the U.S. the displacement of that labor from agriculture is often cited as one of the major faults of a farm system that tends toward large-scale, highly mechanized units.

The rationale for the mechanization and enlargement of U.S. farms has generally been expressed in one word: *efficiency*. That word commonly means getting the most output for the least input. In order to keep food abundant and cheap, it must be produced as cheaply as possible. To do this, it makes sense to replace the expensive inputs with cheaper ones. Since both land and energy were still very cheap in the mid-part of our century, farmers looked for technologies that used more energy and land, and required less labor. Thus there was created a market for large tractors, pesticides, and herbicides, and large-scale harvesting equipment.

One characteristic of these technologies is that they require large amounts of capital. While the Farm Credit System and other government and private lenders could make capital available to smaller farmers, the large operators with access to larger amounts of capital at lower interest rates enjoyed an inherent advantage in adopting these technologies.

There has never been consensus among analysts of American agriculture that these larger farms *are* more efficient. In fact, every study of this question by the USDA has reached the same conclusion: the fully mechanized one- or two-operator farm achieves all of the efficiencies available to larger units. Why, then, do farms get larger than this? The answer was provided in a 1973 USDA report, *The One-Man Farm:* "The chief incentive for farm enlargement beyond the optimum one-man size is not to reduce unit costs of production, but to achieve a larger business, more output, and more total income."

However, the wide acceptance of the need for greater "efficiency in agriculture" (meaning more mechanization and less labor) has consistently caused the Congress to encourage in various ways the flow of capital into agriculture. Among the more effective were tax provisions giving advantages to those who invest in agriculture or who suffer losses due to such investments. Since the taxable income of individual farmers tends to be too low to benefit significantly from such provisions, it was the non-farm investors or corporations that were able to use these options to best advantage. In fact, according to University of Minnesota economist Philip Raup, the growth of large-scale and corporation farming, a relatively new development, was not the result of a need for capital in agriculture. He points to federal credit and tax policies as "an attempt to equip non-owner/operators with bid power in the farmland market" and, Raup adds, "we have witnessed a phenomenal growth in the demand for tax shelters in farming and real estate." [4]

Thus it is argued that the largest farms, particularly those owned by non-farm investors or corporations, are farming the tax system rather than the land. While we are still in a time of surplus, both in food output and in the land necessary to meet the food needs of our people, that situation may change. The structural question is whether farming based on returns to capital investment rather than returns to family labor provides the same food security for a growing world population indefinitely into the future.

Conservation and Land Policy

The third test of modern agriculture is whether it encourages preservation of the food-producing resource. This is a further application of the principle that the land must be cared for to meet the needs of all. Future populations on this planet are also part of the total human community for which our religious and national traditions place responsibility on the present generation.

The need for soil and water conservation appears obvious today. But it is only in our recent history that conservation has received serious attention. As noted earlier, the abundance of good and cheap land made soil depletion a minor concern to America's farmers. It took the dust-bowl experience of the 1930s, with clouds of dust from western farmland darkening the skies of eastern cities, to raise soil conservation to the level of a national concern.

Since the mid-1930s, the Soil Conservation Service of the USDA and numerous government cost-sharing and private efforts have sought to make preservation of the soil and clean water an integral part of U.S. agriculture. As recently as 1978, however, the SCS reported that erosion was depleting topsoil twice as fast as it could be replaced and that agricultural pollution was adversely affecting water quality in two-thirds of U.S. river basins.

The link between erosion and water pollution was analyzed in a 1979 Pulitzer Prize winning series by James Risser of the *Des Moines Register*. He wrote:

So far, any effect that soil erosion may be having on crop production has been masked by the growing amounts of fertilizer applied to the land.

Then, quoting an official of the Environmental Protection Agency, Risser notes that, by volume, "erosion and sediment are the biggest agricultural pollution problem, but the most serious problem is the toxic chemicals, because of the possible health hazards."

The heavy use of fertilizer and the use of large-scale machinery which exposes more soil to erosion and is less suited to conservation practices such as contour plowing and terracing, can in part be attributed to the emphasis on capital-intensive, large-scale techniques. Comparative studies show that smaller scale, more labor-intensive farming tends to be more protective of the soil and less polluting of water. This is partly a consequence of the technology used and partly the result of an attitude.

As Wendell Berry says in his beautiful book, *The Unsettling of America,* it makes a difference whether a farmer is a husbandman or a businessman. A good husbandman-farmer, he says, is a cultural product of experiences and relationships "that are deliberately and carefully native to their own ground, in which the past has prepared the present and the present safeguards the future." [5]

Attitudes toward conservation of soil and water, and the retention of land in agriculture, are likely to reflect the intentions which motivate the landowner. An investor seeking speculative gain from the land is more likely to support conversion of the land to non-farm uses. The annual conversion of some three million acres of farmland to other uses is a consequence of more than just urban expansion and other intensive demands. There must also be a willingness on the part of the owner to release the land from agriculture.

Quality of Life and Land Policy

A fourth test of current farm trends concerns the quality of life of our people. It asks whether large-scale agriculture enhances family and community life or whether a quality life is protected better by a small farm structure. It is difficult to apply specific measures to this question, but one can learn something from the experience of churches that minister to farm communities.

In a 1958 policy statement, the General Board of the National Council of Churches concluded that national

policy should have as a goal the "preservation and extension of the efficient family-type farm as the predominant pattern of American agriculture." The rationale given for this position was that the family farm has provided "that type of rural environment most conducive to the growth of human personality, the stability and enrichment of family life, and the strength of the community and its institutions."

Similarly, the Committee on Social Development and World Peace of the U.S. Catholic Conference in 1979 issued a statement on the family farm, noting that "the farm environment encourages the development of patience, self-reliance, a simplicity of outlook and the particular bond that comes when father and mother and children join in earning their common bread."

The one published effort to analyze the comparative impacts of industrialized and family-scale farms on rural communities was conducted by an anthropologist in two central California communities in the 1940s. This study by Walter Goldschmidt was updated in 1978 by a team sponsored by the State of California. Their findings basically confirmed Goldschmidt's conclusions of 30 years earlier: that the small-farm community was supporting twice as many local businesses and that median family income and retail trade were both significantly higher in the small-farm community, which also had more physical facilities, social services, schools, parks, playgrounds, and churches than the community based on large-scale, mechanized agriculture.

Thus, in all four areas of questioning—the protection of individual rights, the common good, stewardship of resources, and quality of life—the evidence seems to indicate that small-farm agriculture is in greater conformity with the traditional values and the physical, social, and psychological needs of the American people. As noted earlier, however, the economic and political forces at work in America today are rapidly moving us toward an agriculture based on large-scale highly mechanized farm units. Our 150,000 largest farms comprise only 5.3 percent of our total farms but own 26 percent of our farm acreage (1974). It is clear that the trend is far advanced. Can it be slowed or reversed?

Toward New Public Policies

Possible actions fall into two categories: public policies that can be promoted through the political process, and organizational efforts that can be undertaken by groups of farmers and consumers at the local level.

Some of the public policies are most appropriately pursued at the level of state and local government. Others require federal action. All require an orientation toward smaller scale, family-type farms as the basic production unit.

One category of legislation that addresses the trend toward bigness consists of laws that control or limit participation in government farm programs by large operators or absentee investors. Numerous reforms in the farm program to direct its subsidy benefits away from the largest, most financially secure operations and toward the smaller farms are possible and being discussed. Similarly, the credit and loan programs administered by the government for farmers could be adjusted to focus mainly on the needs of smaller operators. Choosing a cut-off point at which farms would be considered too large to participate is the most difficult aspect of these efforts.

Also in the category of disincentives to larger operations, it is possible to prohibit certain interests from engaging in farming at all. There has been legislation before Congress for many years which would make it a violation of antitrust laws for large non-farm corporations to engage in agricultural production. Several state legislatures have already passed laws which make it illegal for corporations other than family-farm corporations to own and operate farmland. Strict enforcement of the Reclamation Act of 1902, long abused by corporations and large farm operators, would restrict the benefits of federally subsidized irrigation water to smaller farms.

A second category of public policy involves providing incentives for farmers to remain small. Until now, tax incentives aimed at assisting farmers have been of greatest benefit to the largest operations and to absentee investors. Those provisions of tax law could be rewritten to assist family scale resident owner-operators. Likewise, the orientation of government-funded research has been toward technologies which require more capital and more land to be used economically. Such research could be redirected toward more labor-intensive techniques that operate most efficiently on smaller-size units.

A further incentive could be provided by state and local governments in framing property tax laws that benefit smaller units. Such laws might base the rate of taxation on the size of the unit, so that owners of smaller acreages pay lower taxes per acre than larger owners. Such a "graduated land tax," a cousin of the graduated income tax, has been proposed in a few states, but is not yet effectively implemented.[6]

A third area of public policy is one of assisting new farmers to get started or to obtain land. Recent changes in inheritance tax laws at the federal level and in some states have addressed one need in this area. High estate taxes have often forced families to sell inherited land in order to raise the cash demanded. Lowering the tax rate on farmland permits the land to stay in the family so that another generation can take over and continue the operation.

One relatively new concept in helping farmers get started is to provide government assistance for the purchase of land. This has been proposed in various forms at state and federal levels, but generally it consists of using government resources to guarantee loans for the purchase of land or to have government purchase land directly and lease or sell it to prospective farmers.

Since entry of new farmers is made more difficult by

the diminishing supply of farmland and the consequent rise of prices, another key area of public policy is farmland preservation. As interest in the protection of farmland has spread across the country, numerous programs have been undertaken. The federal government can assist these efforts with some funding and technical assistance, but such efforts tend to be most effective when sponsored by local and state governments in response to local growth needs and the nature of local agriculture. In addition, governments can take steps to preserve the water supply needed for agriculture so that small producers are not excluded from that essential resource.

All these policy efforts—putting controls on the largest and the absentee-owned farms, boosting small farm income, assisting the entry of new farmers into agriculture, and protecting agricultural resources—are consistent with values that can be traced back to the religious and philosophical bases of western civilization. They challenge certain economic practices and public policies that have emerged relatively recently in our history.

Government policies, particularly federal farm programs and the federal income tax, have such a pervasive influence on American agriculture that a significant redirecting of current trends could not be achieved without revisions in these laws. There are, however, a number of things that farmers themselves, and farmers in cooperation with consumers, can do to improve the incomes of smaller operators.

What Farmers Can Do Directly

Farmers have a long history of organizing themselves into cooperatives, commodity groups, and general farm organizations. This history can be a major resource in efforts to strengthen small farm agriculture in America. For example, farmers can organize marketing cooperatives or join collective bargaining organizations in order to set their own price on what they produce. Through such structures they can in many areas market directly to consumers through farmers' markets, buying clubs, or roadside stands. Bypassing the food wholesalers and distributors saves on the final cost of the product, permitting farmers to charge a little more and consumers to pay a little less. (See Chapter 10.)

Small farmers can gain some of the economies of scale enjoyed by larger operators by buying supplies through their own cooperatives. Buying in larger quantities at one time usually reduces the unit price of inputs. Farmers can further reduce production costs by adopting techniques that require fewer inputs to be purchased. Some farmers experimenting with biological and organic techniques, for example, have been able to reduce their fertilizer purchases without losing net income.

The long history of farmer organizing to protect land and water resources is one that can serve farmers well today. Weed control districts and soil and water conservation districts have long been vehicles through which farmers share the cost of preserving land productivity. Such districts are still important ways of holding down some costs and keeping land and water in useable condition. In some communities, land owners are even experimenting with land trusts as a way to maintain land in certain uses for an indefinite period of time.

The success of organizing and public policy efforts depends to a large extent on the availability of information and the effectiveness of education. The four general farm organizations—the American Farm Bureau, the National Grange, the National Farmers Union, and the National Farmers Organization—along with a new advocacy group called the American Agriculture Movement all conduct major educational activities for their members and for the public. There are opportunities as part of these activities for small farmers to shape the policies of these organizations and to reach large numbers of people with information about their situation.

This chapter began by noting that agriculture depends on two factors: the land and the relationship between people and land. The richness of our nation's land and, throughout most of our history, its abundance in proportion to our population have been major factors in the development of our national life. The relationship between our people and the land is the product of an evolution in our thinking and experience. Our religious and national traditions are less immediate to us than our experience with a changing land policy, but they are still part of the total framework out of which we approach questions of ownership and use of productive land.

Today the main factor influencing that people/land relationship is probably technology. Our infatuation with how quickly a four-wheel drive tractor can plow a field or how a plant responds to large doses of chemical fertilizer sometimes distracts us from the role of the land in the productive process. Many commentators have faulted our society for losing sight of the importance of the land in our personal and social lives. Author Louis Bromfield was one of these. Writing in *The Land* in 1942, he said:

> We were taught unfortunately that automobiles and water closets had something to do with civilization. They have nothing whatever to do with civilization. Civilization is something far above and beyond mere mechanics. Civilization is always, fundamentally, closely related to nature, to God and to the land. . . .[7]

The fact that from the very beginning of our country land policies were made by elected representatives of all the people suggests that we consider the land of America as belonging to all of us. How it is owned and how it is used are matters which we decide as a nation, either by establishing certain policies such as the Homestead Act, or by choosing to take no action. In either case our land policies are a reflection of our people and their sense of what American civilization is all about.

Notes

1. Alexis de Tocqueville, *Democracy in America*. Quoted in Eugene McCarthy, *America Revisited* (New York: Doubleday, 1978), p. 97.
2. Frederick Jackson Turner, "The Frontier in American History," speech to the American Historical Association, Chicago, July 12, 1893.
3. Paul Wallace Gates, "The Homestead Act," *An American Primer* (New York: New American Library, 1966), p. 411.
4. Philip Raup, "Some Questions of Value and Scale in American Agriculture," *American Journal of Agricultural Economics* 60 (May 1978): 307.
5. Wendell Berry, *The Unsettling of America* (New York: Avon, 1977), p. 45.
6. See Byron L. Dorgan, "The Progressive Land Tax, a Tax Incentive for the Family Farm," April 1978 paper for presentation to the North Dakota Legislature. Available from State Tax Commissioner, State of North Dakota, Bismarck, N.D. 58505.
7. Louis Bromfield, *The Land* 2 (no. 2, 1942):154-156. Quoted in Russell Lord, *The Care of the Earth* (New York: New American Library, 1962), p. 292.

For Discussion

1. Compare the quotation from Thomas Jefferson with Lev. 25:23 (opening of Chapter 4) and with the phrase "the Lord's land." How do the ideas differ? How are they the same? Do you accept the author's interpretation of Genesis concerning the three principles related to the land?

2. The author discusses a tension between the ideas of common heritage and private ownership. Is it a creative and constructive tension? To what extent is the land a common heritage? To what extent should it be subject to private ownership? What are the limits to each understanding?

3. A complete study of the biblical view of the land appears in Walter Brueggemann's *The Land* (Fortress, 1977). Could your group conduct a Bible study around these themes related to the land?

● land and limits to our acquisitiveness—resting the land, honoring it, allowing it to have rights (see Amos 8);

● land as arena for justice and freedom (see Isaiah 5 and Micah 2);

● land as promise to the landless and sign of God's faithfulness in covenant (see Gen. 17:8; 35:12; Deut. 8:7-10; Jer. 32:21-23).

4. U.S. farmers have achieved a high productivity per worker-hour. Some other nations have higher productivity per acre or per unit of some other input, such as petroleum. Why have different nations developed their agriculture in different ways? Which is more "efficient"? Does your definition of "efficient farming" lead to different policy goals than those proposed by the author?

5. To what extent should our farm policies promote the following? Rank them from one through four in importance.
● enhanced family and community life
● the principle that property is intended to serve the well-being of all
● preservation and conservation of the food-producing resource
● protection of individual rights

6. Discuss the public policies suggested by the author. If your group is made up largely of food *producers,* invite some retailers, advocates for low-income persons, or others of differing perspectives to talk over these policies with you. If you are from an urban or suburban congregation, invite several farmers to join you. Get beyond the pleasantries and try to understand how specific policies would really affect people in different situations.

6

Strengthening
Rural Communities

by Robert Riedel and Jon Wefald*

It seems that rural areas are more conducive to fostering certain values. Stewardship is one of these. Being close to the earth and being dependent upon nature tend to develop a sense of the earth and its resources as gifts from God to be taken care of and shared. . . . Rural people seem to have a great sense of independence. This makes them very difficult to organize, but with careful guidance could lead to true interdependence. They also seem to particularly value family life and honesty. . . . Rural people, especially farmers, also have a great disdain and mistrust of government.

SISTER JAN CEBULA
From *Rural Issues and Their
Connection with Urban Life*

---

* ROBERT RIEDEL is professor of psychology at Southwest State University in Marshall, Minnesota. JON WEFALD is president of Southwest State University and a former Minnesota Commissioner of Agriculture.

For most of its history, America has been rural. For most of American history, farmers and rural people were regarded as the backbone of the Republic. The urban industrial revolution in the post-Civil War era would slowly transform America. More and more people would leave the land and small towns for the burgeoning cities all across the nation.

But the major out-migration of people from rural to urban America came in the post-World War II period. Indeed, over 30 million people left farms and rural communities for urban industrial America between the end of World War II and the early 1970s, one of the largest migrations of people in the history of the world. The number of farms and ranches dropped from roughly six million in 1945 to barely 2.6 million in 1979. The number of people living in rural America declined from over 50% of the population in 1920 to only 30% by 1970.

The population shift from rural to metropolitan areas continued unabated through the 1950s and 1960s, but began to reverse itself in the 1970s. The numbers tell the story vividly. During the years 1965-1970 there was a net out-migration from non-metropolitan areas of 350,000. But during the years 1970-1976 there was a net *in*-migration of 1,600,000.[1]

The major factors contributing to this change are the decentralization of manufacturing, the development of rural recreation and retirement areas, and a rejection of the big-is-better world view so dominant in urban industrial America.[2] The 17 most rural states gained in population from 1970 to 1973. Meanwhile, of the 10 most urban states, only California, Maryland, and New Jersey showed gains and these were down considerably from the previous rates.

Without downplaying the importance of the factors just listed, it is also important to realize that recent national polls by Harris, Gallup, and Roper note that Americans are increasingly showing a preference for small town or rural residence. Fuguitt and Zuiches have shown that the first choice of Americans is a small city near a big city, while a more remote rural area is second choice.[3]

Halpern indicates that one of the nation's priorities must be to spread population to a multitude of small towns, rural communities, and rural mini-cities.[4] Brown, McGrath, and Stokes identify 22 negative factors associated with current and continued population growth and centralization—including pollution, inflation, environmental problems, inadequate housing, climate change, poverty, crowding, water problems, and unemployment.[5]

The Shortchanging of Rural America

Although 30 percent of the people live on farms and in small towns, rural America has been over the years and still is exploited, neglected, and unfairly treated. For example, with 30% of the total population, rural America has 44% of the poor and 66% of the substandard housing. Yet it receives only 27 percent of the federal outlay for welfare and poverty. Over the past generation farmers and ranchers have consistently received farm prices at or below the cost of production. Rural branch rail lines have been abandoned. Local units of government at the township and county level have been shortchanged.

Moreover, rural areas receive only 17% of federal spending for employment and manpower training programs. Importantly, more than 36% of the nation's population 65 and over resides in non-metropolitan areas, but those areas receive only 25% of the federal outlays for social security and retirement programs. It has been well documented that the smaller the population areas in which the elderly live, the poorer their housing.[6] Compounding all of these inequities, rural America has only 12% of our doctors and 18% of our nurses.

Even in education rural America is shortchanged. About one-third of all students in U.S. public schools are enrolled in rural school districts. Yet the Office of Education and the Department of Health, Education, and Welfare provide rural schools only 5 percent of research dollars, 11 percent of library and materials funds, and 13 percent of basic vocational aid funding. Incredibly, there is not any division or bureau within HEW to serve rural school children. Indeed, there is not one single federal employee in the Office of Education designated a rural school specialist—to relate to the needs of the 33% of all American school children who are enrolled in rural districts!

Today a person can major in urban studies in over 130 colleges and universities in this country. There is really no fully integrated program in any state university where you can actually major in rural studies, even though rural America has over 70 million people. No wonder federal agencies repeatedly hand down decisions and propose rules and regulations that result in the closing of too many farms, rural post offices, rural branch lines, rural hospitals, rural schools, and rural businesses!

One of the reasons for rural America being short-changed too often by government and other institutions is that for the past 50 years we have been producing a great and impressive variety of urban specialists—in education, housing, transportation, poverty, health care, etc. But few, if any, major universities have been training young men and women as *rural* specialists and experts in these fields, young men and women who would come back to serve the small towns of America. As the late Senator Hubert Humphrey of Minnesota said:

> The truth is that rural America, with the exception of a few of us who want to take up the burden, is forgotten. I mean most of the people in government come out of the . . . great universities, they get a fine, good education, and by the time they are through with it, what they knew about rural America has been flushed out and they come back with an entirely different set of values and thinking.

At Southwest State University in Marshall, Minnesota, we are putting together a Rural Studies Program that will integrate scholarly research and teaching in such areas as:

- rural history
- rural society
- agribusiness
- cooperatives
- rural school systems
- rural economics
- rural government and administration
- aging in rural settings
- appropriate technology
- rural music
- values, virtues, and behavior in rural life
- ethnic variations in the rural world
- the future of rural America
- research and development programs for the countryside

What Needs to Happen?

The time has come to develop a critical understanding of our rural values and institutions and what they mean to the future of America.

Southwest State University wants to help train young men and women as future leaders for rural America. We want to develop future doctors, dentists, farmers, business men and women, grain elevator and agribusiness leaders, cooperative managers, clergy, educators—all to play a role in revitalizing rural America. In order to have a healthy rural America in the future, we need to attract more of the outstanding young men and women from our rural areas to remain as future leaders. This is one important way to restore health and prosperity to rural America.

Equally important, we need a prosperous and healthy agriculture. We have to keep independent farmers and ranchers on the land. That takes consistently fair farm prices. How important is agriculture?

Agriculture is America's largest industry.

Agriculture is (after people) our nation's most valuable resource—not oil, gold, platinum, or even uranium.

Agriculture is the greatest single contributor of new wealth and earned income for our national economy. It is the key not only to a favorable balance of trade and payments for America, but a balanced budget as well.

Agriculture is, moreover, the growth industry in America today.

Indeed, American agriculture sets the pace for world production of food and fiber.

No other nation on earth annually produces the volume of food and fiber that we do. American agriculture leads the world in the production of red meats, milk, eggs, turkey, chicken, total poultry meat, processed vegetables, feed grains, soybeans, citrus fruits, and tobacco, and is second only to the Soviet Union in wheat.

In 1978 according to the latest federal estimates, American agriculture produced 65% of the world's soybeans, 30% of its feed grains, 17% of its wheat, 25% of its pork, 15% of its cotton, 60% of its turkey meat, 30% of its beef and veal, and 14% of the world's milk.

We normally export well over half our wheat, about half our soybeans, one fourth or more of our feed grains, one-third of our cotton and tobacco, and one-fifth or more of countless other crops. Export sales are vitally important to agriculture and to this nation's economy.

In short, agricultural export sales for the U.S. are as important as oil exports are for the Middle East. The selling of American agricultural products domestically and internationally at consistently fair prices is a major prerequisite for a healthy rural America.

Toward a Fair Share of Industry

Another important factor in the revitalization of rural America is that it get its fair share of relocated commerce and industry. Industry is beginning to migrate. Fabrication and assembly plants, as well as those involved in raw material processing, such as food, steel, and aluminum plants, are looking increasingly beyond the confines of large cities and their suburbs when they consider building new facilities. Less-urban areas are eager to attract industry. They will often subsidize new industry to locate in their area through direct payments, lowered taxes and utility rates, and even a favored position regarding financing, laws, and regulations.

These small towns, which subsidize or in other ways attract industry, are in a rather ironic position. For example, sometimes a new industry increases the local cost of living substantially, hires few local persons, and generally brings in new residents from metropolitan areas. A case in point is the locating of a large Kaiser Aluminum plant in Ravenswood, West Virginia.[7] The plant was attracted to Ravenswood by the presence of relatively cheap land and taxes. There were no other (and this remained true until at least the beginning of the 1970s) manufacturing jobs in the entire county, so the impact of Kaiser was understandably immense.

Jackson County, in which Ravenswood is located, lost 16% of its population from 1940 to 1956, while the town of Ravenswood remained fairly stable in population at just over 1000. Unemployment was higher than the national average as a result of the decline in agricultural activities in the area and was increasing. The unemployed were usually farm laborers or smaller farmers who needed off-farm work to supplement meager incomes. Thus they were often undereducated and underskilled relative to an urban population.

When Kaiser moved in it had good intentions of hiring local persons first. But it soon became obvious to

Kaiser officials that the typical unemployed person in Jackson County did not meet even their relatively low minimum educational standards. The quality of the job opportunity, however, was such that Kaiser could attract able applicants from relatively far away. This led to a lack of incentive for lowering their standards and hiring local persons. Indeed, it may have actually caused them to have higher local standards than they had nationally. So the local unemployed were "shouldered" out by the migrants who in turn increased the cost of living in the area as a result of the rapid growth.

Ironically, some small businesses in the area were forced to close. After a lengthy period of decline, many of the local small businesses were unable to expand to meet the growth due to inability to find financing. Large chains inevitably were attracted by the area's growth, and their presence soon caused other small businesses to close.

Part of the irony is that small-town chambers of commerce go out to sell businesses on locating in their areas, in hopes of gaining economic benefits for the people and businesses that are already there. Sometimes these towns do end up benefiting economically from the new industry. But they also may end up more like the big cities from which they are attempting to be different.

There is an inherent rejection of the quality of smallness or rurality in the very attempt to attract new business, especially when this occurs simply for the sake of growth, rather than with some overall goal of community betterment in mind which takes into account the effect on the life-style, quality of life, and environment of the current residents.

Another phenomenon that can occur in a sparsely populated area when a new industry moves in is that the local workforce is "creamed." "Creaming" means that the new industry, which usually pays better than local jobs, attracts the cream of its workforce from local firms.[8] This happened when PPG Industries moved into Mar-

shall, Minnesota, the home of the authors of this chapter. The pay scale that PPG could pay was considerably higher than the scale of most jobs in the area. PPG was immediately able to attract local workers to their plant and to attract persons from quite long distances to relocate in Marshall.

There are both differences and similarities between the Ravenswood and Marshall situations. The Marshall experience was similar to Ravenswood in that a national firm was locating in a largely rural area which had, as a region, shown a population decline for some period of time and which had a lower level of pay than was typical for other locations of the company's plants. PPG also brought in an excellent cadre of trained, experienced workers to fill the level of foremen and higher positions, and to do the initial training and supervision.

While many differences from Ravenswood could be listed, we will restrict ourselves to a few we think are particularly important. One is that the level of education in Marshall is higher and a college is located in Marshall; this gives impetus to the growth of the town and local businesses, which have been more able to benefit from the new industry rather than be displaced by it. The region as a whole had virtually no unemployment when PPG decided to move in, and other industry was present which offered some alternative employment. Nevertheless, it is generally agreed that PPG initially "creamed" at least one segment of the local labor market.

Overall, PPG's effect on Marshall has been highly positive in that it attracted new workers from other small towns and even large urban areas great distances away; these were highly skilled people who became a stable part of the local work force. Their presence has increased the number of service and merchandise-related jobs in the area, causing a growth of the local firms with a service or retail orientation. Thus, it seems, in the Marshall case everyone benefited from the new industry, while in the Ravenswood case there was relatively little benefit for the local people.

When it comes to attracting new industries to rural communities, one of the first things that must be done is an analysis of the impact on the local job market, both immediately and as a secondary growth effect. In a small town where there is a great deal of unemployment, we must ask whether the unemployed workers are suitable for the new industry. If not, are they trainable and will the new industry make this additional investment in the area and its people? In areas like Marshall, which have other industries and low unemployment, we must examine the extent and nature of the "cream" effect and how this touches local industry and the community as a whole.

Other Areas of Need

Rural America needs to attract more of its outstanding young men and women to stay as future leaders.

Rural America needs to get fair prices for the food produced by its farmers and ranchers.

Rural America needs to get a fair share of industrial jobs.

But rural America also has many other needs. They are:

- better medical facilities and more personnel

- improved housing

- increased support for local government

- sharply improved transportation

We also need special sets of regulations and policies designed and promulgated for and in a rural area, rather than from Washington or a state capitol.

We won't know until after the 1980 census, and perhaps not even then, whether there is actually a rural

renaissance under way, as measured by significant population and industrial shifts away from the metropolitan
areas. We have seen enough, however, to cause us both
some delights and some fears that there is a shift in our
direction. We experience delight that we were right about
the return to rural areas, and fear because too much
migration can cause us to grow willy-nilly and become
part of the problem rather than the solution.

We believe we must look at more than just growth.
Growth in itself is not an automatic good. A recent newsletter of the Institute for Social Research states:

. . . many non-metropolitan areas are growing faster than
urban areas. But the natural attractiveness of these areas is
being seriously threatened by hasty development and by the
rapid influx of people . . . the attitudes of the area's residents
reflect a "new mood" concerned with limiting growth and
planning more carefully for it.[9]

There are advantages in living in a city, and we are
neither blind enough nor foolish enough to ignore them.
There are also disadvantages with living in a rural area,
and we freely admit them.

What we do not know is just how much growth and
of what kind causes us to pick up some of the benefits
of the larger areas while losing none of the benefits of
rural areas. We must, in all our future growth plans,
attempt to incorporate the best of the rural and the
urban without canceling out the benefits of either. We
must grow to the point and in the manner that provides
the benefits of a city while protecting the environment
and the advantages of a small town.

The people of rural America are ready to play a vital
role in the rejuvenation of the countryside and indeed
of the country itself. But more outstanding young men
and women will have to locate in the towns and small
cities of rural America. Farmers and ranchers will have
to consistently receive a fair rate of return on their in-

vestment, which will thereby create a base of new wealth and earned income for the nation as a whole.

Rural America must get its fair share of commerce and industries. (More agricultural raw materials should be processed in the rural setting.)

Rural America and American agriculture can be a future source of new alternative energies, such as wind power, solar, alcohol, gasohol, methane gas, and so forth.

Rural America needs more and better medical and health facilities.

Rural America needs its share of tax dollars for its schools, roads, local, municipal, and county governments, the unemployed, the poor, and the elderly. The federal government has still not developed a plan for rural America, even though the Rural Development Act of 1972 was envisioned by the late Senator Hubert H. Humphrey to allow the federal government to work with rural people to build a more prosperous rural America.

Rural people want to get on with the job. They know with half a chance that rural America could play a role in the next generation for the whole nation, not unlike the role rural America played in the 19th century—a place of opportunity, employment, land, freedom, and growth. If rural Americans work together, the pride and confidence of rural people will return and the future of rural America will be ensured.

Notes

1. C. Jack Tucker, "Changing Patterns of Migration Between Metropolitan and Non-Metropolitan Areas in the United States: Recent Evidence," *Demography* (November 1976) 435-443.
2. Calvin L. Beale, "Renewed Growth in Rural Communities," *Futurist* 9 (August 1975):202-204.
3. James J. Zuiches, "In-Migration and Growth of Non-Metropolitan Urban Places," *Rural Sociology* 35 (September 1970):410-418. Also Glenn V. Fuguitt, "The Places Left Behind: Population Trends and Policy for Rural America," *Rural Sociology* 36 (December 1971):450-470.

4. Irwin P. Halpern, "Growth Centers and New Communities," *Futurist* 4 (October 1970):163-164.
5. Lester R. Brown, P. L. McGrath, and B. Stokes, "The Population Problem in 22 Dimensions," *Futurist* 10 (October 1976):238-245.
6. Robert A. Bylund, C. O. Crawford, and N. L. LeRay, "Housing Quality of the Rural Elderly," paper presented at the 31st Annual Scientific Meeting of the Gerontological Society, Dallas, Texas, November 16-20, 1978.
7. Irwin Gray, "Employment Effect of a New Industry in a Rural Area," *Monthly Labor Review* (June 1969):26-30.
8. Ray Marshall, "Manpower Policies and Rural America," *Manpower* (April 1972):14-18.
9. Institute for Social Research, *ISR Newsletter* (Summer 1978):8.

For Discussion

1. The opening quotation is a strong statement about rural people, culture, and values. Do you agree with it? Does it imply anything about city people?

2. The authors cite evidence on the shortchanging of rural America. Others claim our core cities are being similarly neglected. People in the suburbs sometimes complain that their taxes are supporting everyone else. Can all these complaints be true? In your opinion, who are the "haves" and the "have-nots"?

3. Do a case study on the movement of an industry into a developing country. You could start by viewing a filmstrip which discusses such activity in relation to Jamaica and Chile. The filmstrip, "Sharing Global Resources," is available from NARMIC, American Friends Service Committee, 1501 Cherry St., Philadelphia, Penn. 19102; Phone 215/241-7000 (35 minutes). Compare with the effects of the movement of Kaiser Aluminum into Ravenswood, W. Va., and PPG into Marshall, Minn. Ask these questions:
● How can Third World nations and communities such as Ravenswood and Marshall influence the impact of industrialization to maximize the advantages and minimize the disadvantages?
● How can industries and communities work together to achieve their goals, whether in the U.S. or in other nations?

4. In 1974 Third World nations called for a New International Economic Order. Some of the elements of the new order

they seek are: better terms of trade, adjustment of their debt burden, more jobs and income from the processing of their raw materials at home, a stronger voice in international financial institutions, and a larger share of the world's income. Do you see similarities with the needs of rural America as outlined on page 117? How do these compare with the needs of the region where you live?

5. This section has discussed the *structure* of U.S. farming. Do you think the trends are moving that structure in the right direction? If the direction should be changed, what policies could do this?

6. The Congress acts on a new farm bill in 1981. Is there a group in your church or community willing to study farm structure issues, discuss them with farmers, consumer advocates, people representing other points of view, and with your legislators and members of Congress? Are you interested enough to take the initiative in bringing together such a group?

7

Managing the
Land and Water

by C. Dean Freudenberger*

*Land is the living, dynamic bridge where crops con-
vert solar energy to human food. It spans the gap between death and life, between what was . . . and what is
to be.*

NEIL SAMPSON
Executive Vice-President
National Association of Conservation Districts

*Although petroleum presently is generating serious
concern and much debate, the use and abuse of soils are
of greater long run concern to this nation's future security and welfare.*

DR. JOHN F. TIMMONS
Iowa State University

---

* C. DEAN FREUDENBERGER is professor of international development studies and missions at the School of Theology at Claremont, Claremont, California. He is also an agronomist. He
has had extensive experience in agriculture overseas.

Perspective determines whether an issue in our experience is a blessing or a problem. The introduction of an irrigation system into an arid valley appears to some people as a blessing. To others, the prospects of eventual saline seep look like a problem. Or, to the farmer standing at the edge of a field, the crop looks good. To Landsat, a U.S. satellite that records and evaluates the earth's mineral and vegetative patterns, the detection of plant nutrient deficiencies suggests there is a problem. Obviously, perspective plays a determining role in the process of problem recognition and analysis.

To me, our present land and water resource management in the United States appears to be a problem. My perspectives are theological and geographical. Theologically, I carry a sense of responsibility in my experience of freedom. I interpret the reality of human freedom of choosing or not choosing to be responsible for my neighbor and my environment as an expression of God's love and trust. A commitment to responsible freedom on my part is my way of expressing gratitude to God for life in our moment of human history. It is my way of saying thanks for my neighbor and for all the resources of creation that surround and support us.

In addition, the idea of responsibility in freedom enables me to have a sense of concern for the well-being of tomorrow's generations of all life forms. These are theological premises, born out of experience and reason and translated into faith. This theological construct, informed by the ecumenical struggle of the churches during the past 40 years to define the nature of a responsible society, provides me with perspectives on soil and water management issues in the United States today.[1]

Globally, my perspectives emerge from my work in agricultural development ministries in more than 60 countries on all continents during the course of the past 25 years. The stress which human life has placed on the soil and water resources of the planet is overwhelming. It is from these personal geographical involvements and theological orientations that I see our land and water management as a problem . . . a very serious problem.

The Setting: National and Global

In the U.S., soil loss from sheet and rill erosion in the grain states is in the range of 9 to 20 tons per acre per year.[2] A recent bulletin published by the Iowa State Soil Conservation Service displays an image of two bushels of soil for a bushel of grain.[3] Most of us are now aware that the Ogallala aquifer of the high plains has been reduced by 50 percent and the remaining water will be pumped to exhaustion in the next 30 to 50 years.[4] The same thing is happening to similar aquifers in other states. Pumping is at a rate greater than recharge.

Dust storms over eastern Colorado and western Kansas in January of 1977, and the southern San Joaquin Valley in the winter of 1978, reminded us of the dimensions of the problem. We are aware also that, on the average in each year, more fertilizers are required to maintain present crop yields. Daily we read of increasing amounts of agri-chemicals in our water supplies. As a consequence of these recent inputs, we wonder about the possibility of dangerous gene mutations in the soil microbiology.

In order to appreciate the issue of water and soil management in the U.S., we must view it in global perspective. The United Nations held a conference on desertification in 1977 as a part of its series of world consultations on the state of the environment. For the first time I was able to comprehend the magnitude of the problem of soil loss as a result of human abuse. In his address to the conference, the Secretary-General of the UN Environment Programme said:

The present rates of soil loss through erosion may be as high as 2500 million metric tons per year . . . over *one-half a ton* of top soil for every man, woman, and child on the planet.[5]

Globally and historically, we have to admit that humanity has thus far lost the race in its attempt to keep pace with its needs for food and fiber while also preserving its soil resource base. The prospects for the future are awesome.

More than a mere threat, desertification is actively at work. A great many people live in dry lands that are now undergoing the process, and their livelihoods are already affected. Estimates of present losses give rise to a pessimistic outlook, suggesting that the world will lose close to one-third of its arable lands by the end of the century.[6]

With regard to fresh water resources, a similar situation exists. About 1% of the earth's water resources are useful for human and agricultural purposes. Since seven-tenths of the earth's surface is water, this is still quite a bit, but . . .

What humanity had thought to be an inexhaustible gift of nature is no longer that, and must therefore be subjected to rational and organized utilization.[7]

As a major consequence of continued land clearing and reduction of forest resources, voices are being raised about the build-up of atmospheric carbon dioxide. In addition, the relationship of the oxidization of nitrogen fertilizers to the threatened stability of the ozone shield is a second focal issue of the UN Environment Programme.[8] These issues, and the possible impact they may have upon weather systems, were discussed repeatedly at the July 1979 World Council of Churches Conference on Faith, Science, and the Future in Cambridge, Massachusetts.[9]

This, then, is the global setting of the church's concern in the U.S. for soil and water management. Lester Brown, in his essay "The Worldwide Loss of Cropland," articulates the challenge well:

The times call for a new land ethic, a new reverence for the land, and for a better understanding of our dependence on a resource that is too often taken for granted.[10]

Obviously the problem of soil and water management is awesome. It is with a sense of freedom in Christ, transcending mundane loyalties, that we are free to ask such difficult and unpopular questions as these:

● How much longer can we continue "business as usual"?

● In terms of soil and water, what are the real costs of agricultural production and how can they be measured?

● What are some of the basic assumptions about agriculture that we accept without question?

● What are acceptable patterns for soil and water use?

● Are there some general principles that can help us determine better ways of relating to land and water resources?

● How do we calculate our responsibility to the future?

The Biblical Story

Our "Landsat" for viewing 20th-century customs of land use in the United States is the biblical story about land stewardship. I am grateful to Walter Brueggeman's book *The Land*.[11] His inquiries have led him to understand the history of Israel as a history of people and land. It is a strenuous history of promise and problem. The story of the exile is a story of people *without* land. The wilderness experience is a story of a search for the land of promise. The occupation of the land is the story of home and homelessness, possession and alienation.

The very land that promised to create space for human joy and freedom became the very source of dehumanizing exploitation and oppression. The land became the problem. The very land that contained the sources of life drove the kings to become agents of death. . . . The promise became the unbearable problem.[12]

Land for Old Testament people was experienced as a symbol of a promise. In faithful obedience, land was understood to be the foundation of justice and freedom (from fear and oppression), assurance of sufficiency for food, shelter, and clothing, and a place of rest and beauty and peace. Land symbolized the vision of hope of the people held in captivity. Yet in this symbolism—the vision of a better tomorrow—there exists a constant struggle. Grasping for one's home leads to homelessness. Risking homelessness yields the gift of home. But all too often the gift of home causes temptation to possession, which in turn alienates and dispossesses.

Thus land is not designed for emancipation. It provides rather for rootage. It does not provide for meaning to the same degree that it gives a sense of belonging. Land does not separate us from community. To the contrary, it gives us location within a community.

Land is never simply physical dirt. It is always physical dirt freighted with social meaning derived from historical experience.[13]

It was the constant temptation of Israel to forget these realities and to *lay claim* to the land. The people laid claim to the land, and in time they lost their land! Are there parallels in our moment of history?

Land Management: Three Biblical Ideas

Three fundamental principles about land management emerge in Old Testament history. The first is that land is *a gift in covenant*. It is always to be managed as the arena of justice and freedom. One cannot take and possess the land. It is not to be disposed of. Israel had no absolute claim. The land was for the well-being of all people of all generations. When the vision of justice is ignored, the land is endangered and can be taken away. Land provides opportunity for expressing responsibility. We are responsible to use the gift of land in ways that are coherent with the covenant to maintain justice and freedom. As Yahweh gives gifts, he also makes claims. He has made us trustees of his gift of land, which is to be used for these purposes. If the land is not cared for it turns to dust—a sign of a broken trust.

The second principle about land management is that it is *of God's creation,* not of our own doing. Land is of intrinsic value in its own existence. Repeatedly, biblical writings suggest that *land has rights* in relation to the people. These rights deny humanity the freedom to exploit the land. The concept of the sabbatical period of rest (fallow) is central to this notion.

The third principle is that land is *a corporate gift* to the people; it is not given to individuals. The Levitical laws about providing land for the landless in the year of Jubilee demonstrate this conviction. Over and over again land is seen as a promise for the people, the basis for their continual freedom from oppression and physical need, and for rest and beauty. Woe to the nation whose kings own the land! We are a people of the land. Out of the dust we were created. We shall return to the dust. Our origin and destiny are inseparable.

One can conclude from the study of Old Testament traditions that our use of the land requires that we never forget it is (1) a gift in covenant, (2) of God's creation and not ours, and (3) a corporate gift for the welfare of the whole community, today and always. We are simply sojourners, traveling with a sense of responsibility and thanksgiving for the land. We are recipients of this fundamental gift of life and its accompanying promise of beauty and peace. We receive this gift in covenental relationship from the Promiser who does not stand outside of history but who is faithful in history. This is our faith and hope; it is also our judgment.

The Gospels talk of the coming of a new age, the new kingdom of God on earth—on the land. Is this gospel a vision or a scandal? To lay claim to this as a vision of promise, Christians must struggle for the achievement

of a just and enduring society. Today Christians must struggle to encourage contemporary science and technology to focus efforts on the welfare of people for generations to come and for the renewability of the land which is of absolute importance to this future. Basic to this vision is a sustainable and just pattern of land use. But, to date, the historical record of achievement of this vision is indeed scandalous, particularly in terms of water and land stewardship. Can a positive chapter in the record of loss still be written? Do principles of biblical tradition about our covenant help us evaluate prophetically what is, and point to what yet can be?

Dangers: Soil Loss

On Sunday, November 26, 1978, Secretary of Agriculture Bob Bergland was interviewed by James Risser of the *Des Moines Register* on *Face the Nation* (CBS Television and Radio Network) :

Mr. Risser: Mr. Secretary, there's quite a bit of evidence that the intensive agricultural production policies of the U.S. over the last couple of years are taking a tremendous toll in terms of soil erosion and depletion of water supplies. Can we continue our present intensive agricultural production without eventually wearing out our resources?

Mr. Bergland: We cannot. We're on a collision course with disaster. . . . Our water supplies are being reduced, we have whole watersheds where the ground water reserves are being depleted, and we have mined our soil. In fact, the erosion of America's farmland today is probably at a record rate, and this simply cannot go on.[14]

Cropland deterioration with the consequent depletion of water resources is not new. What is new is the *scale* of loss, affecting rich and poor nations equally. Soil fertility is now declining on an estimated one-fifth of the world's croplands.[15] The United States is a part of this reality. For example, the organic content of our midwest soils has declined about 50 percent in the last 100 years.[16]

Pressures on the world's croplands have escalated, especially since the middle of this century. In 1950 there were 2.5 billion people in the world. Today there are more than 4 billion. If current UN projections materialize, there will be 6.3 billion by the end of the century. The worldwide pressure for food, fiber, and other resources of the land impacts the U.S. severely. The danger signs of reaching the limits in the U.S. are clear.

In its 1975 nationwide survey, the Soil Conservation Service indicated that annual soil losses on cropland amounted to almost 3 billion tons, an average of 9 tons per acre.[17] In the same year, an Iowa State University experiment station reported, "The 200 million tons of soil lost from Iowa's cropland each year . . . cannot be replaced within our lifetimes or those of our children. The eroded soil is gone."[18]

Dangers: Water Loss

Like the soil, water resources are overstressed. Lester Brown writes:

In the western Great Plains—Nebraska, western Kansas, Colorado, and Wyoming—the withdrawal of underground water now often exceeds the rate of natural recharge. As water tables fall, pumping costs rise, until eventually farmers can no longer afford to irrigate. Efforts to develop the extensive coal resources of the northern Great Plains and the oil shale resources of western Wyoming and Colorado will divert more water from agriculture. In Montana farmers are battling energy firms in the courts in an effort to retain water for their fields. And Denver's expanding water needs are being met by the diversion of water from central Colorado farms.[19]

The *Los Angeles Times* reported (March 1, 1979) that Governor Brown's administration was seeking to alleviate an expected groundwater shortage in California's San Joaquin Valley of two million acre-feet, which would likely expand to a six million annual acre-foot overdraft by the year 2000.[20] The valley's aquifer has 80 million acre feet total.

John Fischer, former editor of *Harper's Magazine*, describes the mining to exhaustion of the Ogallala aquifer of his home area on the high plains. Fifty percent has been used during the past 25 years, and the remainder will be exhausted in the next 30 to 50 years at present rates. This would finish off a water resource that took five million years to develop.[21]

Ross Toole, in his moving account, tells of similar trends of depletion and the impact it is having on the land's people in Montana and the Dakotas.[22] He asks us to ponder some tough questions. What is the magnitude of stress if 250,000 square miles of land are strip-mined? What happens to water-bearing strata when it is disturbed during coal removal? How much water does it take to generate 36 10,000-megawatt coal-fired electrical generation plants? How much is 4.4 million acre-feet of water? What will be the impact of all this on the build-up of atmospheric carbon dioxide?

We can hardly fathom all this. But whether we like it or not, these are the kinds of questions that confront us and that enable us to see the historically unprecedented dimensions of the soil and water management issue today.

Dangers: Land and Water Quality

In expanding the west side of the Central San Joaquin Valley in California, the Central Valley Project annually brings 5 million acre-feet of water to the westlands. Along with it comes 2 million tons of salt accumulation, the equivalent of enough to cover 1800 acres of land one foot deep. It will take about $11 billion and 100 years of work to complete a network of nearly 300 miles of drainage canals, salt marshes, and evaporation reservoirs to control the problem, which in 100 years will involve more than 3 million tons of salt annually. Some 400,000 acres are presently enduring stress. Soon, a million acres will be seriously threatened.[23]

An additional illustration of similar magnitude can be

cited. By 2000 A.D. the Colorado River Basin Salinity
Control Project, near Yuma, will be pumping 2.8 million
tons of salt and agri-chemical residues into the Sea of
Cortez.[24] Recently the Senate Appropriations Committee
heard testimony that the nation's waterways will never
be clean enough for fishing, swimming, or drinking, if
the federal government fails to assist farmers in controlling agricultural runoff. A clean water program's cost?
$10 billion.[25]

It appears clear that we cannot continue our present
manner of agricultural production without eventually
wearing out our resources. Mr. Bergland is not alone in
his "collision course with disaster" warning.[26] Pope John
Paul I, in his address to the College of Cardinals, said,

The danger for modern man is that he would reduce the earth
to a desert . . . introducing death where God wishes life.[27]

Hopeful Signs of Arresting the Trends

During the Sahelian drought of 1968 to 1973, the
World Food Conference of the United Nations in 1974,
and the depletion of world food stocks through greatly
increased purchases of grain by the Soviet Union, little
organized attention was paid to the issues we are discussing in this chapter.

During the latter half of the 1970s, however, global
attention shifted heavily to the question of resource
loss. The UN Environment Programme has helped articulate the global problem. In the past several years, UN-
sponsored conferences on desertification (1978) and water resources (1977) have given new attention to the agricultural resource questions. The UN conference on agrarian reform (1979) related the issue of resource management to land control.

Within the United States, environmental groups have
become more aggressively organized to address the issues
of soil and water management. So have local and regional groups of farmers and ranchers. There has been a pro-

liferation of Protestant and Roman Catholic conferences on issues of rural America. State councils of churches have intensified work on land and food issues. Perspectives from the rich traditions about land and water use from Indian Americans have been especially helpful in focusing the nature of our crisis.

Timely new journals, such as *Acres U.S.A.* and *Ag World,* have come on the scene. Groups of concerned faculty and students in the agricultural schools of our universities are addressing the problem in more determined ways. Such movements as the National Coalition for Land Reform and National Land for People are impacting social awareness and Congressional debate. Leading newspapers are carrying feature articles and lengthy series on soil and water use and abuse.

We know that widespread awareness is the basis on which next steps can be taken. Obviously, until there is a clear social demand, appropriate action is difficult to take. The demand is growing. I am encouraged.

Efforts are fragmentary. Information is hard to find. The broad picture is nearly incomprehensible. Vested interests are deep. Mythologies about the efficiencies of our agricultural system and the limitlessness of our land prevail. We often feel paralyzed and discouraged. But there are signs of arresting the trends. What, then, can we do? The remainder of this chapter will suggest some of the bases for policy that individual Christians and churches might support.

A Sustainable and Just Agriculture

The global dimension of the crisis in soil and water management commands us to find ways to turn the course of this history. Fundamental to policy formation for an agriculture for tomorrow is a renewed understanding of the meaning of agriculture.[28]

The purpose and goal of agriculture is to provide good nutrition for human beings and creative employment for those who work the land. Human potential can unfold in communities of dignity which live in harmony with the natural environment. A regenerating agriculture is basic to all strategies for achieving anything in human endeavors. For agriculture to work, and for civilization to survive, the critical equation of balance between the earth's soil and water resources and its vegetative cover must be maintained.

Within this frame of reference, a policy concept for agriculture suggests that it be *sustainable and just.*

A *sustainable* agriculture means that its technologies can be repeated indefinitely and without loss. Sustainable agriculture implies that its technologies are structured around solar and biological energy and that its resource inputs for food and fiber production are renewable.

A *just* agriculture means that whatever ecologically appropriate technologies are applied by one person or community of persons to grow food and fiber can be practiced by everyone in similar circumstances, indefinitely. Justice in agriculture applies, of course, to the large issue of the availability of support structures for individual farmers and their communities.

This policy concept is difficult to implement in the midst of today's proliferation of technologies, with their heavy dependence on nonrenewable resources. E. F. Schumacher reminds us:

One of the most fateful errors of our age is the belief that the problem of production has been solved. This is an illusion . . . mainly due to our inability to recognize that the modern industrial system, with all its intellectual sophistication, consumes the very basis on which it has been erected. To use the language of the economist, it lives on irreplaceable capital which it cheerfully treats as income.[29]

So we ask: what are the practical steps? What should we do to move in the direction of a more sustainable and just agriculture? I have five suggestions.

1. A Science of Limits. The prevailing commitments of agricultural science and technology have been absorbed mainly with the questions of the expansion and maximizing of production. But the evidence which has been submitted above suggests that it is time to look at the limits of things.

What are the limits to soil and water use? What are the limits of the oxidization of nitrogen fertilizers with reference to the stability of the ozone shield? What are the limits to prevailing fossil-fuel-energy technologies for food production, processing, and distribution? What are the atmospheric limits to heat absorption and the reflectivity of light as a consequence of land clearing in relation to cyclical climate patterns? What are the limits of mono-cropping, the extermination of insects and soil microbiological life? What are the limits to nitrogen build-up in water tables and the overnourishment of surface water in our lakes, ponds, and streams? What are the limits of tolerance in the carrying capacity of each ecosystem over the long period of time?

Many people argue that we do not have sufficient evidence to answer these questions. They say that until we do there is nothing wrong with keeping on in the way we have been going. There are others, however, who suggest that because of the magnitude of possible impact of what we are doing, we ought to be cautious until we are sure.[30] My experience with the irrevocability of desertification and collapsed rural societies during the past quarter-century suggests the latter course of action. And therefore I ask that we develop an agricultural science that is much more attuned to living with limits.

2. Social and Environmental Impact. Two questions are helpful when developing a cropping technology consistent with a just and sustainable agriculture. First, how does a particular technology contribute to or break down the maintenance of the ecosystem of my immediate as well as the larger environment? Second, how does technology contribute to the process and guarantee of preserving the agricultural resource (soil, water, vegetative cover) for future generations?

These questions may be used for policy formation for the welfare of future generations. Obviously, if our concerns are not future-oriented, then such questions will seem to be nonsense. But if we care about agriculture beyond today, then we will include such questions in our policy basis.

3. Bio-Intensive Agriculture. An insight currently re-emerging is one that our grandparents understood well, but which we have neglected in North America for the past generation. It is that agriculture ought to be as biologically intensive and sophisticated as we know how to make it.

For example, many of our grandparents were extremely knowledgeable about crop rotation schemes. They may not have understood completely why a method worked, or how Rizobium bacteria in legumes fix atmospheric nitrogen, but they observed that it happens! They integrated animals into their cropping scheme as a vital part of the whole production process.

It is my view that agriculture must move back toward the management practices our grandparents used, but based on as much current theoretical knowledge as possible.

4. Smaller Farm Size. For the past 30 years or so we have been infatuated with the so-called miracles of agri-chemicals and genetic engineering of plants that could respond to these chemical inputs. We have neglected to explore less costly and less risky approaches to viable agriculture. We have been so engrossed with maximizing crop yields and with labor-substituting devices that we have lost track of the role of people in agriculture.

We need to be excited about new possibilities in smaller farm sizes, and to establish new definitions of produc-

tion costs and efficiencies that can be experienced with smaller farms under different management approaches and with intensive biological practices. We can learn from research in other parts of the world, such as the findings in mixed-farming approaches that come from places like the International Institute of Tropical Agriculture in Nigeria.

5. *Food and International Relations.* Finally, it seems to me that until we develop international relationships of cooperation for the development of sustainable self-reliance in food production in the food-deficit nations, we will never get handles on either the expanding food deficits or the expanding deserts. Until the more than 140 food-deficit nations make a transition from colonial export crops, and create the essential rural infrastructure to encourage farmers to produce for the goal of sustainable self-reliance for their own community and nation, their people will remain hungry and agricultural environments and resources will continue to deteriorate. This job cannot be done without international cooperation.

Within the few food-exporting nations, the trend toward soil and water resource exhaustion will not turn until there is a throttling back of high production in food and feed grains. It is obvious that soil resources, as rich as they appear to be, cannot maintain the kinds of yields being achieved currently. One part of the world cannot feed the other for very long. Every nation needs to work toward a policy of sustainable self-reliance, though a good deal of trade in agricultural products will no doubt continue. But the poor nations must certainly produce more food crops in the future, and that will mean a decline in agricultural production for export (coffee, tea, cocoa, rubber, tobacco, sugar).

We are part of a global food system today, just as we have a single worldwide ecosystem. People on the land all over the world are participating in and responsible for the maintenance of the whole biosphere, for now and for the future. There is no substitute for international planning, consulting, and cooperating.

Land is a gift in covenant. It is God's creation, not ours. It is a corporate gift for all generations. As Christians who are trustees of this endowment, we have freely accepted the invitation to achieve justice and sustainability in the management of the land and its water resources.

Let us understand the limits to which the resources of the land can be stressed.

Let us always measure the impact of our technologies against the concepts of renewability and social justice.

Let us expand the application of what we understand in the area of biointensive cropping systems.

Let us study the possibilities of reducing farm size.

And let us expand our capacities for cooperation internationally, to reduce the need for food imports on such a large scale, strengthening the self-reliance in food and fiber of the poorest nations.

An Illustration

Is a just and sustainable agriculture possible, or is it wishful thinking? Perhaps an illustration can challenge the imagination.

One bright Sunday morning during my sabbatical study leave in the spring of 1977, my wife and I decided to take a short trip into the British countryside. We walked to the bus stop in our adopted village of Piddinghoe, in southern England. The village was built in the 12th century. It is perched picturesquely on the edge of the Sussex Downs. Downs are rolling hills covered with pasture grasses and with oak-lined ravines. We walked down our graveled village road past the post office and pub. Beneath a great oak tree we waited for the bus.

When we boarded we found ourselves among other picnicking families who were on their way to a favorite spot near the sea where farmers pasture their sheep during the lambing season. Arriving at the village of Rottingdean, we followed the nearby trails, specifically designated for hiking and picnicking, onto the rolling fields. To everyone's delight, hundreds of ewes and lambs were grazing, nursing, and frolicking in the warm sunshine. To hear laughing children as they watched the joyful antics of newborn lambs was an added delight.

During previous centuries, most of these hills were covered with brush and oak forests. Long ago, all of that vegetation had been cut for construction purposes and the making of charcoal. But, wisely, the people of the past century had launched programs to rehabilitate the badly eroded hillsides.

Today, although the soil over these chalk hills is still very thin, it is preserved and slowly building up the root systems of the heavy pasture sod. The land is preserved for sheep grazing and for recreational uses by the people of the nearby villages and the more distant cities. Because of the vast network of public transport, these magnificent hills are within easy and inexpensive reach of many people. There is no urban or industrial sprawl. New tax structures and inheritance laws, based on land permanently designated for agriculture, offer no threat to sheep growers. There are no dune buggies, recreational vehicles, or trail bikes.

Instead, there are bicycle and walking paths, kite flyers, laughing children, nearby train stations, and convenient bus routes.

This experience, along with similar ones of justice and sustainability, beauty, harmony, and dignity, which I have encountered in locations around the planet, inspire me with hope for a secure tomorrow for my own nation and for our global community of nations.

To me, security has come to mean something other than safety from hostile attack. The security that I seek has something to do with sustaining the basic resources essential for the guarantees of justice to future generations—guarantees of arable soil, abundant vegetation, a stable atmosphere, good water resources, and sufficient food supplies.

I have hope that we will turn, in time, to tend to those guarantees. The future of civilization depends upon our doing so.

Notes

1. Paul Bock, *In Search of Responsible Society* (Philadelphia: Westminster, 1974).
2. R. I. Dideriksen, "Erosion Inventory—Sheet and Rill Erosion," December 1978, p. 5. American Society of Agricultural Engineers, Box 410, St. Joseph, Mich. 49085.
3. U.S. Department of Agriculture Soil Conservation Service, "The State of Our Iowa Land," Des Moines, Iowa, 1978.
4. John Fischer, *From the High Plains* (New York: Harper and Row, 1978), and Charles Bowden, *Killing the Hidden Waters* (Austin: University of Texas, 1977).
5. M. Tolba (the secretary-general of the United Nations Environment Programme), "The State of the Environment —1977," UNEP/GC/88, Rome, March 14, 1977.
6. United Nations, *Desertification: Its Causes and Consequences* (Elmsford, N.Y.: Pergamon, 1977), p. 9.
7. Luis Jourequi (the under-secretary for water resources of Argentina), in a press release from the UN Water Conference at Mar Del Plata, Argentina, WAT/45, March 14-25, 1977.
8. Tolba, *ibid.*
9. World Council of Churches, Conference on Faith, Science, and the Future, plenary papers on "Science and Technology as Promise and Threat," "Risk Management," "The Transition to a Just, Participatory, and Sustainable Society," and "Limiting Economic Growth," Cambridge, Mass., July 1979.
10. Lester Brown, "The Worldwide Loss of Cropland," World Watch Paper No. 24, Washington, D.C., October 1978.
11. Walter Brueggemann, *The Land* (Philadelphia: Fortress, 1977).
12. *Ibid.,* p. 11.
13. *Ibid.,* p. 2.
14. From an unpublished manuscript of the program *Face the Nation,* with guest Bob Bergland, November 26, 1978.
15. Lester Brown, "The Worldwide Loss of Cropland," p. 5.

16. Michael Perelman, *Farming for Profit in a Hungry World,* (Osmun, N.Y.: Allenheld, 1977), p. 35.

17. R. I. Dideriksen, "Erosion Inventory—Sheet and Rill Erosion," pp. 18-20.

18. Iowa Experiment Station, "Our Thinning Soil," Research for a Better Iowa, February 1977.

19. Brown, "The Worldwide Loss of Cropland," p. 22.

20. *The Los Angeles Times,* March 1, 1979.

21. Fischer, *From the High Plains,* p. 173.

22. Ross Toole, *The Rape of the Great Plains* (New York: Harper and Row, 1978).

23. U.S. Bureau of Reclamation, the California Department of Water Resources, and the California State Resources Central Board, *Agricultural Drainage and Salt Management in the San Joaquin Valley,* Fresno, January 1979, p. 3.2ff.

24. *Ibid,* p. 3.6.

25. *The Boston Globe,* July 21, 1979.

26. See note 14.

27. Pope John Paul I, *Time Magazine* (September 11, 1978), p. 82.

28. For expanded notions on this theme, see Wendell Berry, *The Unsettling of America,* Sierra Club Books (Covelo, Calif.: Yolla Bolla Press, 1977).

29. E. F. Schumacher, *Small Is Beautiful* (New York: Harper and Row, 1975), p. 20.

30. Barbara Ward and Rene Dubos, eds., *Only One Earth* (New York: Norton, 1972).

For Discussion

1. Do you agree with the statement by Dr. Timmons quoted at the opening of this chapter? If not, why not? If so, what can you do about it?

2. The author suggests that we should stop pumping water for irrigation in certain areas of the country where the water table is being lowered dramatically. If we follow such a policy, who would benefit and who would suffer?

3. In Chapter 4 Don Reeves reminded us of the instructions and promise in Lev. 25:18-19. How does that theme relate to the biblical perspective in this chapter? What are the rights and responsibilities of those who hold title to land?

4. "The purpose and goal of agriculture is to provide good nutrition for human beings and creative employment for those

who work the land." Do you agree? Is that now the goal and purpose of agriculture in America, as you see it?

5. Do we really live on irreplaceable capital and cheerfully accept it as income? If so, how? Give some examples.

6. What kind of criteria do we use today to determine farm size and cropping practices? Are these criteria those which will lead us to a just and sustainable agriculture?

7. Is there a short-term price to be paid if we move from current agricultural patterns to a just and sustainable agriculture? If so, who will pay that price? Will it be shared equitably or paid mainly by a few? Are there ways to share the burden?

8. Freudenberger's closing illustration pictures a life different from that which many of us now know. How is it different? Do you find the differences attractive? Should we encourage such changes in the U.S.? If so, how?

8

Energy and Agriculture: A Search for Balance

by Harold F. Breimyer[*]

Agriculture . . . has shifted in a very real sense from soil to oil.

WILSON CLARK
energy specialist
State of California

* HAROLD F. BREIMYER is Perry Foundation Professor of Agricultural Economics at the University of Missouri, Columbia, Mo. He is a frequent writer and speaker on issues in U.S. and international agriculture.

Food is a fountainhead of energy for sustenance of humankind. The production of food is a voracious user of the fossil fuel stored below Earth's crust.

The positive role of agriculture comes from its place in the Creator's ecological design. Agriculture hosts the plant life whose chlorophyll converts the energy of the sun's rays into materials for food, clothing, and shelter.

At the same time, modern agriculture—farming as we know it in North America—is a heavy user of fossil fuel, especially petroleum and natural gas. Almost all the new technology brought to agriculture since World War II has required large quantities of energy—for field power, for manufacture of fertilizer, pesticides and similar materials, and for transport.

In one respect agriculture's two roles are opposite and competitive. It would be much better if needs for the products of agriculture could be supplied without such heavy consumption of depletable fuels. The quantity of fossil fuel used can in fact be reduced, and will *have* to be reduced. More will be said about this obligation below.

But there is a symbiotic relationship too. The newer technologies, energy-using though they be, enhance the energy-capturing capacity of growing plants and therefore add to agriculture's energy productivity. Those technologies act in several ways:

1. The energy of petroleum powers tractors, which have replaced horses and mules. In so doing, approximately 60 million crop acres that formerly produced hay and oats for those work animals are freed for food production.

2. Natural gas is feedstock for nitrogen fertilizer. When implanted near the roots of seedlings, the fertilizer nourishes larger plants that expose more leaf surface to the energy-conveying rays of the daytime sun. Larger harvests of grain or other products result.

3. Fungicides, pesticides, and other applied chemicals reduce crop losses to disease and pests. Hence they add to harvestable yield.

So it is that both scientists and citizens calibrating the progress of modern agriculture take note not only of the size of yields, nor solely of agriculture's appetite for fossil fuels. Instead, they balance the two. For the goal is not just to maximize the former, nor only to minimize the latter, but also to attain a favorable energy-output/energy-input ratio.

To anticipate the ultimate message of this chapter, the admonition is not to take such drastic steps to conserve energy in agriculture as to revert to yesteryear's horse and mule farming. It is instead to modify our present practices to the goal of economizing on use of fossil fuels while still sustaining high productivity.

And to further pre-summarize, if we think in terms not just of farming but of the entire food system, much of the potential adjustment will be found farther along in the system. Even consumers' choices of the kinds of food they eat bear on economy in energy.

Different parts of agriculture and the food system vary widely in their energy efficiency, and choices among kinds of foods and method of preparation can be more conserving of energy than even radical changes in methods of farming.

The Energy-Output/Energy-Input Ratio

As awareness has sharpened of the energy debacle that looms for the United States and other western industrial nations, not only our attitudes have changed but our language too. In agriculture, we no longer talk only about crop yields per acre, or production per person. Increasingly the lexicon includes the ratio statistic that relates the two parts of agriculture's *energy* equation, the energy-output/energy-input ratio. This measures the energy content of agriculture's products relative to the quantity of fossil fuel energy used to produce them.

Because the higher crop yields of recent years have come at the expense of sharply greater energy consumption, the energy-output/energy-input ratio has been decreasing. Years ago, when tractors were only an engineer's dream, the ratio was almost infinitely high. Although crop yields were low by today's standards, the only petroleum energy input was grease for wagon wheels, oil for harness, and kerosene for lanterns. Output relative to that small input was impressive.

In developed nations where energy-using technology now is universal, the energy output/input ratio has dropped precipitously. Even so, the ratio for field crops remains in favor of output. Except for a few fruits and vegetables, farm products return several times as many calories (or BTUs) in the product harvested as were used in producing it. Estimates vary by crop and by location (also by estimator), but, except in areas of deep well irrigation, corn returns two to four energy units for every one unit used in production. Wheat is roughly similar.

Some vegetables have a ratio less than one to one. Their calorie content is low. They may be valuable for their minerals or other nutrient properties, but they fail to yield as many calories as are used in their production.

Agriculture's big negative factor, however, lies in feeding harvested crops to livestock and poultry. Manifestly, all animals require energy to maintain their body functions—even to keep warm—and their meat, milk, and eggs have only a fraction of the energy content of the feed eaten.

Because animal products are big in the diets of U.S. consumers, the energy output/input ratio for all agriculture—crops and animals combined—apparently is a little less than one to one. Agriculture today seems to be a little on the "inefficient" or net loss side in energy conversion.

Nevertheless, animal agriculture ought not be tagged as energy-wasteful in terms that are too categorical. As one reason for caution, the several species differ sharply in conversion ratios. Fish, not land animals, are the most efficient. Fish farming, now substantial in the border states and South, yields about one pound of fish for each pound of the feed that is spread over the surface of the pond. Birds do better than mammals: broilers will eat two to three pounds of feed for each pound of live weight gain. Hogs require twice as much feed as broilers. Beef steers, pampered on corn and protein meal in their comfortable quarters, have double the feed requirement of hogs. Milk cows are now fed so generously that their marginal energy efficiency is also low. (Pound-for-pound feed conversion is not an exact index of relative energy output/input ratios, but does indicate approximate relationships.)

On the other hand, a distinction can be sketched among species of animals—bovines on the one hand, and hogs, chickens, and fish on the other. Beef and dairy animals have four stomachs, well-designed for digesting coarse roughages. To the extent beef and dairy cattle graze ranges and pastures that otherwise would be wasted, they perform a valuable function in yielding food for human beings. It is the *grain* feeding of cattle that reduces efficiency ratios sharply and raises questions about their future place in an energy-conserving agriculture. But as *forage* consumers, beef and dairy cattle can be human benefactors.

Energy Used in Farming Operations

Production of food and feed crops on farms draws on only a small part of the nation's total energy supply. According to estimates of the U.S. Department of Agriculture, only 2.9% of all energy goes into farming operations for producing food.

Cotton and tobacco add somewhat more. The energy

requirement in modern cotton production is rather large, due to sizable acreages that are irrigated with water pumped from deep wells. Also, both cotton and tobacco are fertilized heavily. As noted below, much fossil fuel energy is used in manufacturing nitrogen fertilizer.

The data that follow are confined to the production of *food* crops. Data are more complete for those crops than for nonfoods; in addition, it is instructive to compare energy in producing food with energy used in the rest of the food system.

Of the energy used in farm production of food, the relative quantities are as follows:

fertilizer	31%
field operations	22%
irrigation	13%
farm vehicles	13%
grain handling/drying	8%
livestock care	6%
pesticides	5%
other	2%

The popular image of energy use in farming is of big tractors drinking fuel, barrel after barrel. Tractors and other power equipment *do* account for substantial quantities; yet the internal combustion engine uses energy fairly efficiently. The biggest consumer is manufacture of fertilizer. The Haber-Bosch process of manufacturing nitrogen fertilizer uses natural gas as feedstock. As seen in the table, the quantity is large.

National average data as given above are somewhat misleading. The statistics fail to show how energy-absorbing are certain practices, such as drying of grain and deep-well irrigation in areas where they are common. Reportedly, more energy can go into drying of high-moisture grain than into producing it. Only a part of the irrigated area of the U.S. is deep-well; some is gravity flow. Already some deep-well irrigation has been stopped because of the cost or unavailability of power for pumping the water.

Steps to Be Taken: Practices

Few universal prescriptions can be offered for ways to economize on energy use in agriculture. As one reason, we must always consider not only the usage part of the equation—the denominator—but the numerator of production (energy content of foodstuffs) as well. A second reason for caution is the variation in agriculture in the United States. Few recommendations apply everywhere.

Take minimum tillage (cultivation of land) as an example. It is natural, mere common sense, to suggest shifting to reduced tillage. The practice has in fact spread widely, and to generally good results. On the other hand, it must also be recognized that (1) reducing fuel for tractors is not a big saving of energy; (2) on some soils reduced tillage results in reduced yields; (3) weed control can be a problem and, if more weed-killing chemicals must be applied, little if any net saving may result. So minimum tillage belongs in the repertoire of possible energy-saving practices, but is not always advisable.

Almost equally sensible is economy in use of nitrogen fertilizer. A first suggestion is better salvage and application of animal manure. A second is to plow under green crops, usually legumes, called green manure. This was once common practice. Some agronomists have worked out new combinations of cropping and management that offer promise. In general, the options are wider in mixed crop and livestock farming areas than where cash crops predominate.

One of the most promising opportunities for economy in energy is new methods of grain drying. Just to dry with circulation of air, without heat, is energy-saving.

Solar heat can be employed effectively in drying. The mechanics are under study at several agricultural experiment stations.[1]

In general, the better prospects for attaining economy in farming without sacrificing productivity lie in ancillary activities rather than field operations. Care of livestock is another example. The trend has been toward confinement care of various kinds of livestock and poultry, even, sometimes, with climate control! This extension of luxury to farm animals seems likely to come to a halt, or to reverse. It is profligate of energy.[2]

With regard to curtailing irrigation, already happening in some places, careful management can ease the effect on crop yields. Nonetheless, the overall prospect is that deep-well irrigation will eventually be cut back substantially, with notable reduction in both use of energy and in yields.

No compendium of farming practices can be offered here. Any farmer wanting to contribute to the social goal of energy efficiency and simultaneously save dollar cost to himself can take advantage of information available from local extension and experiment station personnel.

Steps to Be Taken: Legislation

One of the anomalies of our time is that even as economy in use of fossil fuels is advocated, much of our legal structure acts to encourage the opposite.

Two examples are environmental rules and tax laws.

Environmental rules are not as vulnerable to criticism as they once were. In fact, they have been changed over time in an energy-conserving direction. For example, at one time the philosophy about wastes from feedlots, dairy barns, and other livestock or poultry installations centered on safe disposal into waterways. Increasingly, recovery and spreading on soil has received support.

Although some critics regard the pace as too slow, in crop pest control the trend is toward integrated pest management systems, which conserve chemical pesticides and therefore energy.

The clearest instance of conflict is tax law. Although the legislation enacted in 1978 contains some tax write-offs for solar installations and certain conservation measures, by and large tax laws encourage—subsidize—equipment and buildings that are *highly energy consuming*. The most obvious instance is investment credit rules that help finance purchase of big tractors, construction of livestock facilities that often are highly energy-using, and other investments that seldom conserve energy and often waste it. All tax rules that help to finance grain feeding of cattle are energy-wasteful, as grain-fed beef is near the lowest of all foods in energy output/input ratio.

A different outcome results from the terms of foreign trade in farm products. Devaluation of the U.S. dollar has actually been energy-saving! It has been so in the sense that by making export trade more attractive, including export of feedstuffs, it reduces the incentive to feed livestock here at home. Under the stimulus of larger export demand, feeding of feed grains has scarcely changed in volume since the late 1960s. Although consumers may prefer to have more meat, milk, and eggs available at lower prices, our gradual, forced shift to a more vegetable diet is energy-saving.

Energy in the Post-Farm Food System

We must also give brief attention to energy use in the food system past the farm. As has been suggested, processing, distribution, and preparation of food account for much more use of fossil fuel energy than does its production on farms. Estimates of the USDA are as follows —data are the percentage of *all* U.S. energy consumption that goes to the food-related activities shown:

farm production	2.9%
processing	4.8%
marketing	1.3%
preparation	
at home	4.5%
away from home	2.8%
transportation	0.4%

The total is 16.7%. About a sixth of all energy used in the U.S. goes to produce, process, and prepare food. Of that total, less than a fifth represents energy for farm production.

The data bring a host of ideas to mind. They also suggest that a number of changes in the way food is made available will become necessary in the future. To begin with the smallest item, transportation, U.S. consumers are accustomed literally to drawing on the food resources of the entire planet. Coffee and bananas from the tropics are fixtures in our diets. Bostonians put California-grown fresh fruits and vegetables on their tables routinely. We may all find ourselves eating more fruits and vegetables that are produced close to home, and fewer that come a long way.

Grain-feeding of livestock may drift back toward the place most feed is produced, the Midwest. Thereby transport will be economized.

Processing and preparation of food suggest mainly cooking it. Granted that heat is required in both cases, data show that U.S. consumers are hooked on refrigeration. Substantial quantities of food are now distributed in frozen form, and held in household freezers that are a heavy drain on electric current, which in turn is an uneconomical use of energy except in areas blessed with hydroelectric sources.

Even food *shoppers* are refrigerated, though not frozen: most supermarkets, built huge for convenience, are air-conditioned.

Big supermarkets can be energy villains in another

sense. Compared with neighborhood grocers, they are usually located in shopping centers to which customers must drive some distance. Estimates suggest that a shopper driving a large automobile several miles to shop, and buying a modest quantity of food items, will use more energy in travel than was required to put the food on the market shelf, beginning with the farmer.

The mind can be boggled by thinking about ways the food system will change in the future. Best bets are that highly processed foods will be casualties, as will many frozen foods—unless freeze drying (which reduces volume many times) proves practical. Our diets will likely change away from high energy-consuming foods to more energy-saving ones. Highly finished beef is again the most prominent target. The recent trend toward leaner beef will doubtless continue.

Eating out has usually been regarded as a luxury. Yet mass preparation of food is more economical of energy than preparation dish-by-dish at home. It seems almost a contradiction that the trend toward institutional food service, including restaurant dining, will be viewed as economical and may in fact be speeded.

Agriculture's Production of Industrial Energy

All the discussion thus far has centered on the food system. The energy content of food produced in agriculture has been matched against the energy requirements of modern farming. In addition a few data were presented on energy use in the food system past the farm.

But agriculture produces not only food. It produces cotton, wool, and tobacco. Farm woodlots produce timber.

Cotton and wool are not usually thought of in terms of their energy content. They do contain energy, and energy efficiency is an appropriate factor. Wool is a joint product of sheep growing. Cotton is a primary product. Although tightening supplies of fossil fuels will restore natural fibers to more prominence, the cotton situation relative to artificial fibers is far from one-sided. Some cotton is produced with deep-well irrigation. More energy is required to manufacture a man's shirt from cotton than from polyester. Also, artificial fabrics launder and dry better than cotton ones. But again we run into an interesting commentary on the way we live: cotton fabrics compare better with artificial ones if after washing they are *dried in the sun* rather than in energy-using dryers!

Agriculture has always produced a little energy that is directly substitutable for fossil fuels, if only the wood that farm families have burned in their stoves or furnaces. Recently, however, the idea of deliberately producing industrial energy in agriculture has come into glowing prominence. Most publicized has been gasohol, but a whole school of researchers has addressed the subject of biomass. *Biomass* is the production of industrial energy biologically.

The logic is clear. Growing plants can convert solar energy into materials for industrial processing, even as they already do in timber for burning, in rubber trees, and in a selected few other instances.

Gasohol is a gasoline/ethanol blend, usually 9:1, that burns well in automobile engines. Most has been produced from grain, by a distillation process that is scarcely different from production of whiskey. Following fermentation it requires large quantities of heat to boil off, literally, the alcohol from the water. Research data compiled to date indicate that more energy is required in the distillation than is obtained in the alcohol that is produced.

But preoccupation with gasohol could divert attention from the many other ways in which plant materials could be transformed into an industrial form of energy. Wholly new kinds of plants might be raised for the purpose. Fast-growing trees might make swampland suddenly productive and valuable. Or some of the emphasis might be on recovery of waste materials, even animal manure.

A few ingenious farmers have set up methanol converters for producing their energy needs on their own farms. Although a problem may arise in matching supply with utilization, a significant aspect is that production of energy from waste materials is a localized activity. It is possible that a viable biomass system will be essentially decentralized, in sharp contrast with centralization in cities (congestion, some would say) that has marked the growth of industry using fossil fuels.

An Epilog

The final word in this essay must warn against casual or careless prediction—against what is sometimes called extrapolating from the present. New territory is being explored, conceptually and operationally. Agriculture, like the rest of our economy, has never felt a moral obligation or economic pressure to economize on fossil-fuel energy. On the contrary, the move has been to adopt cultural practices that add to gross agricultural output but almost always increase the energy requirement. When energy was plentiful and cheap, that attitude, while perhaps short-sighted, was not illogical.

Clearly, during the 1970s a reckoning came to America. It came with a jolt. Comfortable citizens were not prepared for it. They suddenly learned that the God-given resources of our planet divide into (a) those that, *with prudent stewardship*, can be perpetual in nature ("flow"), and (b) "stock" resources that are depletable and in process of being depleted. Some fossil fuels are being depleted rapidly.

We U.S. citizens have not yet regained our equilibrium. No prospectus for living with a changed energy situation has yet been drawn up. The ideas offered here are therefore partly conjectural. In what direction we will go is hard to predict. There is only one verity: our nation, including its agriculture and food system, will necessarily make major adjustments. These will take several forms. They will include conserving energy throughout the food system, in production, processing, and preparation. Also involved will be a search for new sources of energy, including energy produced in agriculture.

A collateral moral also is pointed to. If energy-using materials that have enlarged the productivity of land resources in the past will be scarcer in the future, it will be mandatory to guard, protect, and conserve the land with a degree of stewardship not previously known. Productive farmland is not now being protected well. Millions of tons of silt-clay loam float to the bottoms of streams and into oceans each year. In the interest of survival, our nation cannot allow this loss to continue unabated.

It is noteworthy that the message of this chapter has been couched in general terms rather than as a favorite scenario such as "ecological agriculture" or advocacy of smaller-scale family farms. In many respects attentiveness to efficient use of energy in agriculture *will* militate in favor of environmentally sounder farming practices and units of modest size. More integration of crop with livestock farming; incorporation of more organic matter into the soil; crop rotation to minimize both insect and weed losses, in place of monoculture—these and other energy-efficient techniques are better adapted to farms of moderate scale.

Yet those techniques are not limited to family farming. Moreover, and inversely, reestablishing a family farm agriculture would not alone assure efficiency in use of energy or conservation of soil. Family farming's record is not that good. Family farmers have often gone into specialized cropping, without livestock. Family farmers have plowed up terraces because their tractors were too big. Family farmers have not joined wholeheartedly in correcting the non-point pollution of water. Even though family farming may have some implicit advantages, issues in the use of energy in agriculture and the food system can't be simplified into unbridled confidence that family farming holds the magic key.

This chapter ends without a pat prescription but with a warning comparable to that of an Old Testament prophet. Energy must be conserved, as must land, timber, water, and other resources. In our tradition, this must be done within the democratic tradition. Unless our nation can demonstrate its capacity to do so, the outcome will be not evolutionary accommodation but revolutionary turmoil. Democracy itself could be a collateral casualty.

Notes

1. The Small Farm Energy Project, Box 736, Hartington, Neb. 68739, is also working on alternative technologies for both conserving and *producing* agricultural energy.
2. The presence of livestock on a grain farm can also represent a saving of energy, since grain consumed by on-farm livestock does not require a massive amount of grain drying.

For Discussion

1. Look again at the table showing percentage of all U.S. energy consumption that goes into food-related activities. At which points in the entire process are *you* directly involved? How can *you* reduce the energy consumed in any of these activities? The author suggests that changes in the way food is made available will become necessary. How will these changes affect you? Is that good or bad? Will you find it difficult to adjust to such changes?

2. "It is possible that a viable biomass system will be essentially decentralized, in sharp contrast with centralization . . . that has marked the growth of industry using fossil fuels." What are some of the social and economic implications of changing from centralization to decentralization? Let your imagination run: what would life be like if, instead of importing tomatoes from Mexico and energy from Canada or the Middle East, most of what we consume were produced within 100 miles of our home and most of our waste were recycled within one mile?

3. "Energy must be conserved, as must land, timber, water, and other resources. . . . Unless our nation can demonstrate its capacity to do so. . . . Democracy itself could be a collateral casualty." Is the author correct? If so, should you and your acquaintances, your church, your community do something more about conserving resources? What should you do?

9

Chemical Dependency: Can We Break Our Addiction?

by Argyle Skolas[*]

It is possible to substitute pesticides for land, unless, of course, it costs more to kill the pests than to lose the crop they destroy. It is possible to substitute water for land, diesel fuel for land, new genetic stocks for land— all of these, but only up to a point. And many believe industrial agriculture as practiced in Western nations has reached that point.

CHARLES LITTLE
President of the American Land Forum

---

[*] ARGYLE SKOLAS and his family operate an 80-acre diversified farm near Westby, Wisconsin. They produce beef and grains with a negligible use of chemicals. Argyle is active in global and domestic hunger programs of the American Lutheran Church at local, state, and national levels.

It is clear that U.S. farming depends heavily on chemicals of all types. Among these are chemical fertilizers and pesticides for crops, plus preventative and curative medicines and synthetic growth-inducing feeds for livestock.

A look at a few statistics will indicate the degree of chemical consumption in American agriculture. Use of nitrate and phosphate fertilizers in the most recent years has averaged 50 million tons,[1] and the cost of such fertilizer exceeded $6.6 billion for the 1975-76 year.[2] Annual expenditures for drugs and chemicals used in livestock production equals 5% of the annual gross receipts from farm livestock, or approximately $2 billion.[3] During the calendar year 1976 we used 661 million pounds of pesticides.[4] Some analysts conclude that our use of pesticides will double within the next 25 to 30 years.[5]

The increasing use of chemicals in farm operations is but one aspect of the pervasive change in farming philosophy that has occurred over the last 30 years. And if consumption is any indication, U.S. agriculture appears to be definitely hooked on chemicals. For purposes of this discussion, our questions are:

- _Why is U.S. agriculture heavily dependent on chemicals?_
- _Why is that chemical dependency detrimental?_
- _How can the dependency be lessened?_

I. Reliance on Chemicals Has Increased as Farmers Have Expanded and Specialized

Farming in the United States traditionally was a diversified operation, incorporating a variety of crops and several types of livestock, all within the management of one farm family. Farming has evolved during the past 30 years into a highly specialized operation involving substantially larger amounts of land for each individual farmer. Expansion and specialization go hand-in-hand,

and the greater emphasis on one requires a larger dose of the other. One effect of this expansion and specialization has been a massive reduction in the farm population, and a consequent erosion of small towns, small businesses, small churches, and other institutions in America's rural communities.

At the same time, agribusinesses that provide the inputs for expanded specialized farming, the machinery and chemicals, have promoted this evolution. Expansion and specialization require a shift from labor-intensive farming to capital-intensive farming. Technology to support this shift has been viewed as inherently good. For example, technological innovation has allowed the cultivation of marginal land, land which would be fit only for pasture or hay without use of modern technology and new products. A significant part of the technology allowing cultivation of marginal land has been chemical fertilizers and pesticides.

Cost-efficient farm production justifies the use of chemicals, to some extent. But the excessive use of chemicals in agriculture results from many factors unrelated to cost-efficient production—or to any other real benefit to either the farmer or the future of farming. Most of the factors increasing agriculture's dependence on chemicals relate simply to the way agriculture has evolved in recent decades. Thus, to understand the causes of our chemical dependency, we must examine the bases for the increasing specialization and expansion of farming operations.

1. Production for Its Own Sake. Through the drastic changes in agriculture in the past 30 years there has been little regard for efficient use of our natural resources, protection of our environment, the rising cost of production, or the deterioration of rural society. The main emphasis has been on production for its own sake.

Higher production does indeed lead to a higher gross income. But farmers can still lose *net* income in two ways: (1) overproduction cuts the price of marketed products and (2) the incremental increase in cost of production may exceed the incremental income—that is, beyond a certain yield, the cost of producing an additional 10 or 12 bushels per acre may be greater than the income from those extra bushels.

Expanding production has meant not only increasing per-acre yields, but also increasing the number of acres farmed by any one farmer. As farmers expanded their operations they also specialized their operations, concentrating their efforts on a particular kind of farming. Whereas farmers previously fed a major portion of the grain they raised to their own livestock, grain and livestock operations have become increasingly separated and specialized. With specialization in grain farming on some farms comes specialization in livestock on others.

Specialization seems to have begun in the poultry business in the 1950s. Farm feed and equipment companies developed the technology for large units of broiler and egg production. This in turn provided an opportunity for other farm input firms to sell special equipment, feeds, drugs, financial credit, and so forth. Next the technology for large-scale hog confinement operations was developed. The confinement situation gave birth to its own set of animal health difficulties, requiring the use of ever-increasing amounts of drugs and chemicals. Soon, automation provided opportunity for off-farm investors ("Wall Street Cowboys") to enter large cattle-feeding operations as limited partners who realized a major portion of their return in the form of income-tax benefits.

Specialization of poultry and livestock in large units is closely related to the $2 billion in drugs and chemicals used annually in livestock production. Such large units for livestock and poultry production serve to shift farming of all kinds into greater specialization. Prior to the specialization, midwest farmers fed a large portion of their grain to their own livestock. Animal wastes were used as fertilizer on diversified farms, but became a disposal problem for feedlots and large-scale confinement operations.

Not everyone has forgotten the value of animal wastes. The Montford Feed Lots in Colorado now trade one ton of manure for one ton of silage with their neighboring grain farmers. Unfortunately, this is a rare example of the proper use of animal wastes by large-scale feeders.

2. *Influence of Agribusiness.* Agribusiness, most notably the petrochemical industry, has influenced farmers and the public generally by capitalizing on some basic American notions. Among these are "bigger is better," "capital and technology will solve our problems," "without chemicals the world would starve," and the much overstated "American agriculture is the most efficient in the world." (According to a recent report by the General Accounting Office, "Changing Character and Structure of American Agriculture: An Overview," by some measurements we are a very *in*efficient agricultural system. The amount of food produced per farmer is not a true measure of efficiency; the cost in use of nonrenewable resources must also be pumped into the equation.) [6]

In a growth-oriented economy, we all find a sense of security in the theme constantly emphasized by agriculture and agribusiness—that capital-intensive operations and constant expansion provide the solutions to all problems.

The influence of agribusiness is highly pervasive. Most directly, there is continual advertising through all forms of media, depicting the ideal farming operation as one which utilizes large amounts of machinery and chemicals. Advertising is an essential part of our economic system, but must be understood for what it is: privately financed propaganda. And the people who have pushed expansion and specialization in farming for their own business reasons have had something they wanted to sell which that kind of farming had to have.

A more subtle influence of the agribusiness industry is found in the farm publications which make their major profit from advertising revenues. It is not surprising that the articles and research findings printed in farm publications emphasize the type of farming that creates the most business for the publisher's advertisers.

3. Orientation of Research. Further, the research projects of our own colleges and universities have been oriented toward higher technology, often assisted by business contributions to research funds. A professor's degree, tenure, and standing in the professional community all relate to his or her ability to do research and publish. There are substantially greater sources of research funding for projects which would *increase* the use of agribusiness products than for those which would emphasize a low-overhead approach. Thus researchers have a natural bias toward high-technology research. Such research tends to support expansion and specialization in farming operations.

4. Availability of Credit. Easy credit is another source of expansion and specialization in the agriculture industry; thus it contributes indirectly to the heavy use of chemicals. Agribusiness and the federal government are major suppliers of this credit. The equipment companies have their own finance plans which provide income from both sales and interest. The futures markets give the farm producer an opportunity to hedge his production and gain more borrowing power.

But the greatest monetary impetus for expansion has probably been inflation. Inflation has made more credit available for expansion and specialized equipment purchases by increasing the farmers' equity in their property, thus increasing their borrowing power. Further, the closer the inflation rate comes to equaling the interest rate, the lower the true cost of borrowing capital.

It is not always by choice that a farmer specializes or

expands. Often lending institutions encourage it. Some government loans even have acreage requirements that encourage more borrowing and expansion.

5. *Government Policies.* Perhaps the most influential factors in promoting farm expansion and specialization have been our nation's public policies. Agribusiness has learned that the millions it spends lobbying in Washington brings a high return for the money spent. Besides, cheap food has always been good politics. Everyone wants cheaper food, leaving more money to be spent on other forms of consumption. The government's policies have encouraged growth in farm size, in programs such as these:

● spending millions on research programs to aid large-scale farm operations;

● providing price supports in a way that benefits most those who need help the least—in 1975, the 16% of farms with highest incomes received 47% of government payments;

● writing tax laws that underwrite growth, through depreciation and capital-gains benefits, investment credits, and so forth (as noted above, many large-scale cattle feeding operations were founded as tax-sheltered limited partnerships to take advantage of special tax benefits available until 1977).

In recent years the high cost of oil imports has expanded our trade deficit. In response, the government has encouraged all-out grain production for export. In 1975 Earl Butz, Secretary of Agriculture, told the Senate Committee on Agriculture and Forestry that agriculture had become our leading source of foreign exchange and was a powerful factor in maintaining the economic health of the nation. The Central Intelligence Agency conducted a study in 1977 which concluded that world food shortages could give the U.S. a measure of power that it had never known before. Secretary Butz often referred to our food as an international "weapon."

It is evident that we have been using our agricultural resources and large amounts of chemicals to help pay for our extravagant use of energy and to maintain our nation's political power in the world.

All of the factors we have discussed serve to motivate expansion and specialization of farm operations, thereby increasing agriculture's reliance on chemicals. Yet none of these factors relates to the long-term benefit of farmers, the preservation of farmland, or the efficient use of nonrenewable resources.

II. The Arguments Against Continuing Reliance on Chemicals in Farming

If our dependence on the petrochemical industry for food production continues, the world food situation may become critical. Our current energy problems should alert all of us to the importance of depending more on renewable resources. The dangers of depending on the petrochemical industry were the subject of a *Rural America* magazine interview with Dr. Barry Commoner, professor of environmental science and author. Dr. Commoner said:

The fact that agriculture is dependent on energy leads to a harmful situation in agriculture. Take the use of fertilizer. Nitrogen fertilizer is made from natural gas and represents, for example, 47% of the energy used in the production of corn. Another 19% is propane for drying the grain, and only 18% is for running the machinery. So it would make no sense in going after the 18% used in running the machinery. The thing you have to ask yourself is "what about the fertilizer?"

Even there, it is the economics rather than the energy conservation that is important. The dependence of corn production on inorganic nitrogen fertilizer means that the farmer is now dependent on the petro-chemical industry for a very important input. The use of ammonia in the U.S. is divided just about evenly between the farm and the petro-chemical industry, because it is an important ingredient in chemical synthesis. It is also produced largely by the petro-chemical industry. So you have the farmer competing with the petro-chemical industry for this very important ingredient, but it is something that the petro-chemical industry itself makes. . . .

. . . In other words, I think it would be good for a corn farmer to become less dependent on the use of ammonia. But the reason for it is not to save energy for the country; it is to make his operation less dependent on the economic dominance by the petro-chemical industry.[7]

A look at the fertilizer industry amplifies Dr. Commoner's concerns. The following is from a U.S. Department of Agriculture report:

Fertilizer producers face serious uncertainties on both the cost and revenue sides of the industry. Construction costs of many types of fertilizer facilities have skyrocketed. The availability and costs of natural gas and consequently the feed-stock cost for manufacturing anhydrous ammonia is uncertain. The production cost of fertilizer is tied to the government's energy programs, which in turn directly affect the availability of natural gas. Pollution control costs may also reduce or eliminate the profitability of present or future facilities.[8]

Transporting and hauling of chemicals has also become a serious concern. Derailments and tank leakage have caused evacuations in some communities. Disposing of chemical wastes creates serious problems. More government money, more supervision, and more regulation are required to protect the public.

Some analysts predict that we will double our use of pesticides and other agricultural chemicals within the next 25 to 30 years. But there are factors which could change that. One is the increasing cost of pesticides and fertilizers. Another is the increased evidence of ill effects on our environment and our personal health. For such reasons, the Environmental Protection Agency has already banned the use of several pesticides. The EPA is actively reviewing the benefits and hazards of several pesticides now being marketed, and has identified 45 others for similar review.[9]

The Food and Drug Administration is withdrawing approval of several drugs used as additives in livestock feed, including the hormone additive DES.

Furthermore, studies show that where pesticides are used with greater intensity, crop losses due to pests frequently increase. Thus it appears that the utility of chemical pest control as a practice may be declining.

We need to begin reducing agriculture's chemical dependency before it is too late. Agriculture must avoid the situations that have arisen in the areas of transportation and generation of electricity. In transportation we spent nearly $100 billion to build superhighways for trucks and autos, while ignoring the more energy-efficient railroads. We built interchanges and complex highway systems in our cities and ignored the energy-efficient mass transit systems. We now need mass transit and quality rail transportation desperately.

Consider the example of nuclear power. Nuclear energy was imagined to be a cure-all to our energy needs. But our failure to develop energy from other renewable sources leaves us facing the problems of nuclear generating safety and nuclear waste disposal without feasible alternatives.

Agriculture must take a second look at its chemical dependency and its related commitment to capital-intensive, large-scale operations. Taken to its extreme, our present direction could lead to far greater government controls and even to a land reform policy. Roger Blobaum, agriculture consultant to both governmental and private clients, puts it this way:

It is clear that the resource-exploitive, energy-intensive agriculture that now provides our food and fiber cannot endure in its present form. A nation that continues to live off its resource *capital*, instead of utilizing a sustained system that makes it possible to live off the *interest*, is in deep trouble.[10]

We must ask whether we shall continue to use large quantities of fertilizers and other chemicals for all-out production in order to balance our trade deficit. It should be realized that the food we export is directed mainly to other developed nations, not to feed the hungry of the earth. Peter Rogers, professor of environmental engineering at Harvard University, disputes the idea that the best approach to world food security is for the *developed* countries to make large increases in food production. He says:

I don't believe this is a very careful way of approaching world food security. Such a policy destroys the incentive for developing nations to become agriculturally independent. There is no point in dumping tons of food into poor nations except during times of emergency.[11]

It appears that there will need to be major changes in agriculture's approach to farm operations. Research and development must be directed toward farming techniques that rely on greater use of renewable resources. U.S. farming must move away from capital-intensive technology, including chemical dependency. I believe that the transition is inevitable. We should begin changing direction as soon as possible.

III. How Can We Move Toward Less Chemical Dependency?

There are already some hopeful signs that we may be changing. Some 80% of the USDA insect and plant disease control budget is now directed toward fundamental biology and non-chemical methods of pest management.[12] A University of Illinois agronomist, Ellery Knake, has said that chemicals may become less important in the future as the trend toward stricter regulation of chemicals increases. He explains that integrated programs of pest management have become popular in many parts of the country as a means of reducing environmental hazards and dependency on extensive spraying programs. Knake predicts that in the future more farmers will encourage certain plant diseases that attack only the weed and not the crop—or will use chemicals that occur naturally in the environment to attack weeds.[13]

Texas A and M University has developed a new short-season cotton variety for the lower Rio Grande Valley. Using integrated pest management in the irrigated areas, this short-season cotton was grown without pesticides, with less irrigation, and with less fertilization than conventional practices required.[14]

University of Wisconsin bacteriologist Winston J. Brill reports that certain varieties of tropical corn are lending themselves to development of a strain that obtains nitrogen from the air and therefore requires less nitrogen fertilizer. His findings point to the possibility of obtaining agriculturally significant levels of nitrogen fixation in corn. Within five years he hopes to have developed a bacteria strain that will supply at least 10% of a corn plant's ammonia.

The minimum tillage and no-till methods for corn production are regarded by soil conservationists as helpful in controlling erosion. But this approach requires a greater use of pesticides and fertilizers. As indicated earlier, nearly three times as much energy is used to produce nitrogen fertilizer for corn production as is used to work the soil. Thus, energy efficiency may actually require larger amounts of tillage.

Fertilizer consumption in the U.S. and Puerto Rico during the year ending June 30, 1978, was 47.6 million tons, down 8% from the 51.6 million tons consumed during the 1976-77 year.[15] While using 8% less fertilizer, we nevertheless had record grain yields in 1977-78, suggesting that the utility of additional increments of nitrogen fertilizer has been overrated.

USDA studies show that as we increase nitrogen fertilizer, the yield per additional pound decreases. Yet some county agents still tell us that "for every dollar you spend on fertilizer, you get back three dollars." They should be saying, "Be careful, after a certain point every dollar you put into fertilizer may give you back only fifty cents."

Dr. Barry Commoner states:

Studies compared organic farms in the corn belt areas that don't use any nitrogen fertilizer at all with conventional farms. In our two-year averages, the income from crops per acre on organic and conventional farms is identical: about $133 per acre. These are mixed crop/livestock farms. If you look at the yields, they are slightly higher on the conventional farm, about 10-12%. Also, the gross incomes are higher. But the *net* incomes are the same because the expenses are lower on the organic farm due to the enormous cost of chemicals.[16]

However, the new technology of plant life and pest management, the banning of some pesticides, and the outlawing of drugs in feed additives will not substantially cut our use of nonrenewable resources under our present scheme of farm operations. Diversification of farm operations is still the most important step in decreasing our dependency on chemicals.

Diversification has many aspects. Those most significant to reduction of chemical use are (1) integration of livestock into the operation and (2) use of crop rotations which include nitrogen-fixing legume crops.

I believe we must return to an emphasis on smaller, diversified family-type grain and livestock farms. There are many advantages in them, and the other writers in this book deal with several. Let me mention two that relate to reduction of chemical dependency:

1. Diversified farming allows farmers to duplicate nature's cycle to restore the land with a minimal reliance on chemicals. Crop rotation schemes can use legumes to increase the nitrogen in the soil (U.S. farming uses only one-third as many nitrogen-fixing plants as we did 20 years ago). The use of animal wastes as fertilizer reduces the need for heavy use of commercial fertilizer and pesticides. In some cases, with proper management, the use of chemicals can be eliminated.

2. Where farm operations are diversified, livestock are

kept in smaller units, lessening animal health problems. The concentration of large numbers of poultry, hogs, or cattle creates a number of health difficulties that even drugs and chemicals cannot correct. Currently, an amount equal to 5% of total farm receipts from livestock production is being spent on drugs and chemicals for livestock.[17]

Diversification has a number of additional advantages, not related to the use of chemicals, but worthy of note:

● less time is spent in transporting equipment and produce between farming operations;

● it lessens the risk arising from weather and price fluctuations;

● it brings the farming family into more direct and personal involvement with the operation. Confucius is reported to have said, many centuries ago, "The land-owner's footprints are the best fertilizer."

World Food Problems and Diversification. The question of whether U.S. agriculture can reduce reliance on chemicals turns on a much larger issue. That issue is whether specialized grain production in the U.S. is the long-term solution to world food problems, or whether such production is simply being promoted by special interest groups, including our government, for short-term political and business gains.

We should remember that expansion of the food supply may be had through increased livestock production as well as more grain production. It is ironic that many of the same people who encourage our using less feed for livestock in this country—in order to feed a hungry world—are also encouraging grain exports, much of which goes to feed livestock in the rest of the developed world! When we consider the limited amount of land that can be cultivated (less than 5% of the earth's land total) versus the amount that can be utilized through grazing, we can see the importance of ruminant animals to our total food supply. Ruminant animals can convert legume plants into food products. Such plants, notably alfalfa, are also essential to crop rotation schemes through which cultivation of legumes fixes nitrogen in the soil during one crop year, to allow the growing of corn in the subsequent year without addition of commercial nitrogen fertilizer. And marginal land, land best suited for grazing and hay production, can utilize ruminant animals to produce food without being placed into grain production.

Glenn Butts, manager of Performance Registry International, writes:

The cow has correctly been described as the foster mother of mankind. The cow is a self-propelled, self-replacing harvester of grass and forbs unplanted and uncultivated. She converts this replaceable resource into milk and meat that are not approached in their contribution to human health. Your opportunities include sheep and the nonprestigious goat. Witness the spectacular research being done with the latter by the Rockefeller Institute in Arkansas. The contribution to the well-being of uncountable millions of low-income folks and low-energy ecologies cannot be estimated.[18]

Thus our emphasis on specialized grain production is inappropriate to our overall health and well-being. Further, our emphasis on specialized farming generally appears misplaced since such operations do not make the most efficient long-term use of our resources, including the land itself.

It is not that we need to decrease grain production or increase livestock production overall, but rather that we need to merge these two aspects of production into single family-farm operations. The effect of such a change will be to reduce our dependency on capital-intensive techniques, including the heavy use of agricultural chemicals.

An Appeal to Christians. Most farmers will agree that they have a kinship with the land that goes well beyond the relationship of an owner to business property. Humanity's spiritual and social well-being requires humble acceptance of the thought that "The earth is the Lord's and the fulness thereof" (Ps. 24:1). Acceptance of that premise opens the possibility of authentic faith and responsible stewardship. We do not truly own anything, but are trustees of God's possession. The resources of the earth are God's gift to both present and future generations, to be used for the benefit of all humanity. Consider this quotation from an article by Jack A. Nelson:

Land is of special importance. When the people of Israel were slaves in Egypt, they were forced to work the land for others. Then God intervened to free them from oppression and poverty. He led them to "a good and broad land, a land flowing with milk and honey" (Exod. 3:8). To the Israelites, their land was significant because it was a gift from God and because it made possible social relationships based on equality and justice. The biblical writers insist that the use of land reflects a nation's social and spiritual fabric. They make it clear that spiritual health is intimately tied both to the health of the land and to the economic and social health of the community—and that unjust land use is a sign of spiritual, social, and environmental decay.[19]

When we take God seriously and accept our Christian responsibility, we realize that we cannot continue to deplete our resources by abusing and misusing the land. Thus we cannot continue to be dependent on chemicals, while disregarding pollution, health hazards, soil erosion, and endangerment of our future food supply.

Public attitudes need to be changed. We cannot continue to rely upon capital-intensive technology and heavy chemical use. All Christians, not just farmers, must speak in favor of preserving our farmlands, whether they be threatened by overuse of chemicals or by highway commissions and housing developers.

Christians have opportunities to take stands on these matters, but they have often failed to do so. In Wisconsin, for example, there is a farmland preservation act. It is a voluntary program designed to preserve agricultural land and to maintain the agricultural economy, particularly the diversified family farm. By entering into an agreement to maintain the land in agricultural use for five years, farmers receive a refund on their real estate taxes, the amount being determined by the size of their tax and income. Despite this monetary incentive, many farmers, local public officials, and church groups ignore this opportunity to preserve both farmland and diversified farming. There is a lack of public concern.

The farmland preservation act is but one small example of the kinds of policies the churches could be supporting. Congregations could be discussing such policies in relation to our concern for stewardship of the earth. Church members need to support more such legislation on both state and federal levels.

The time has come when church leadership, laity and clergy, must speak up and organize politically in support of this basic meaning of stewardship; total commitment to showing our love for fellow human beings by the wise use of God's gifts, for the blessing of this generation and those to come.

Notes

1. U.S. Department of Agriculture, Economics, Statistics and Cooperatives Service, "1979 Fertilizer Situation," FS-9, December 1978, p. 13.
2. USDA Economic Research Service, "The Changing U.S. Fertilizer Industry," Paul, Kilmer, Altobillo, Harrington, Agricultural Economics Report No. 378, August 1977, p. 1.
3. Walter Wilcox, "Concerns About Chemicals in Food and Fiber Production," 1978 Food and Agricultural Outlook: Papers Presented at the Food and Agriculture Outlook Conference Sponsored by the USDA, held at Washington, D.C., November 14-17, 1977, p. 110.
4. USDA, Economics, Statistics, and Cooperatives Service, "Farmers' Use of Pesticides in 1976," Eichers, Andrilenas, Anderson, Agricultural Economic Report No. 418, p. 4.
5. Wilcox, "Concerns About Chemicals . . . ," p. 110.
6. U.S. General Accounting Office, "Changing Character and Structure of American Agriculture: An Overview," 1978.

7. Barry Commoner interview in *Rural America*, September 1976, p. 4.
8. "The Changing U.S. Fertilizer Industry," p. 47.
9. Wilcox, "Concerns About Chemicals . . . ," p. 112.
10. Roger Blobaum, "Stewardship of Natural Resources," presentation at Farm and Food Issues Consultation, Louisville, Kentucky, February 11-13, 1977.
11. Peter Rogers, *Agri-View* (May 5, 1979), p. 5.
12. Wilcox, "Concerns About Chemicals . . . ," p. 111.
13. Ellery Knake, *Agri-View* (June 2, 1979), p. 17.
14. Wilcox, "Concerns About Chemicals . . . ," p. 110.
15. USDA, "1979 Fertilizer Situation," p. 13.
16. Barry Commoner interview in *Rural America*, September 1976, p. 4.
17. Wilcox, "Concerns About Chemicals . . . ," p. 110.
18. Glenn Butts, "What Is Your Response to 'Where Do We Go from Here'?" *Performance Registry International.*
19. Jack A. Nelson, "Caring for God's Land," *The Lutheran Standard* (June 19, 1979), p. 33.

For Discussion

1. Do you agree that American agriculture is heavily dependent on chemicals? Do you accept the author's reasons for that dependency?

2. Do you agree that such dependence is detrimental? If so, what policies do you consider important in reducing that dependency?

3. What would be the effect of your policy prescription on consumers? On farmers? Who else would be affected? How? Would the burden fall unfairly on some group or groups of people?

4. "Humanity's spiritual and social well-being requires humble acceptance of the thought that 'the earth is the Lord's and the fulness thereof.'" What does that mean for each of us?

5. The author writes that public attitudes need to be changed. How does that happen? Do we as individuals play a part? Does the church? Can your congregation help to change public attitudes? Can you?

10

Direct Marketing:
Is It Coming Back?

by Anna Hackenbracht[*]

He went out again to the market place at nine o'clock and saw some men standing there doing nothing, so he told them, 'You also go and work in the vineyard, and I will pay you a fair wage.'

Matthew 20:3-4 TEV

[*] ANNA HACKENBRACHT is food policy advocate for the California Church Council in Sacramento.

It's only 7:30 on a cool, clear Saturday morning and already hundreds of people have come to buy fresh cucumbers, okra, corn, tomatoes, eggs, milk, beans, apples, breads and peaches from the 30 or so farmers whose trucks are lined up in the church parking lot.

As soon as the crates are unloaded, shoppers begin crowding around to haggle over prices, seek out the best buys, and purchase their groceries. Even though business is brisk, the farmers have time to greet customers, help them choose their produce, and let them know what goods will be coming at the next farmers' market.

By early afternoon more than 300 customers have come to take advantage of prices up to 40 percent less than those in the grocery stores. Most of the farmers have sold out. They return home pleased by the quantity of produce they have been able to sell and the prices they have received.

Such happenings are making a comeback in numerous communities across the country. What these buyers and sellers are part of is direct marketing, an ancient and exciting way to distribute agricultural products. The object of direct marketing is to reduce both the time and the cost of marketing food. In 38 states today there are 782 farmers' markets where consumers may buy directly from producers.[1] That's an increase of 60 percent in the past couple of years.

Marketplaces as Community Centers

The farmers' market is not a recent phenomenon, nor is it the only form of direct marketing. But it is probably the most prevalent form that history has known. It was the original system of food distribution beyond the producer's own family. Shortly after agricultural societies developed in the fertile river valleys of the Nile Delta, a distribution system was established where farmers could set up stalls in a central location of the village.

Often other traders and craftpersons would come to the market to sell and barter. As the communities grew, the markets took on the responsibility of serving as the political and social centers as well as the focus for economic activity.

In the Bible the marketplace is portrayed as the center of public life. When Jesus entered a city, he would often go to the marketplace to meet the people of the town. Many times he spoke at the market. The people knew it was Jesus' custom to visit the market, as demonstrated by the following passage in Mark's gospel:

> And wherever he came, in villages, cities, or country, they laid the sick in the market places, and besought him that they might touch even the fringe of his garment . . . (Mark 6:56).

Other biblical references to marketplaces appear in Matt. 20:3-4; 23:7; Mark 7:4; 12:38; Luke 7:32; Acts 16:19; 17:17.

Today, farmers' markets throughout most of the world remain one of the central institutions of towns and cities. Anyone who has traveled in Africa, Asia, Latin America, and parts of Europe can recall the carnival-like atmosphere, with the noise of barter, the colorful displays of produce and other wares, and the aromas of fresh-baked goods.

In our own country, markets were the common experience until about 30 years ago. Farmers' markets reached their peak in the U.S. during the Great Depression when farmers were desperately trying to save their crops from rotting in the fields and thousands of citizens were anxiously seeking food at prices they could afford. Numerous makeshift stands and markets sprang up all over the Midwest and the Eastern U.S.

Meanwhile, in the West, particularly in California, the years since the mid-1940s have seen a rapid expansion of agricultural production. California, with its highly commercialized farming, has emerged as the nation's leading agricultural state. Ever-increasing applications of machinery, expansion of irrigation facilities, and the availability of cheap, migratory laborers has enabled California farmers to produce a wide array of fruits and vegetables. Grain production in the West was also substantial. The opportunities of vast new European markets, price-support payments from the U.S. government, and good wartime prices spurred production in the West.

A National Marketplace Develops

With the end of the Depression, the number of farmers' markets dwindled rapidly, particularly in the East. At the same time, the giant supermarket chains began to grow. Local and regional markets were soon replaced with the concept of a national market. The western states with their vast diversity and variety of produce fit easily into this new, expansive market. Entry into it was facilitated by cheap energy, which permitted long-distance transportation and technological developments such as improved refrigeration.

To ensure the efficient delivery of large volumes of produce throughout the nation and the world, a regular delivery system and uniform product standards were developed. The establishment of such practices allowed a produce buyer in Minneapolis to be confident that an order of Texas grapefruit, which the buyer had not seen, would arrive on a given day and be of a particular size and quality.

The structure of the existing marketing system is designed to satisfy these requirements. Hence, most products are picked green and ripened under artificial conditions to avert spoilage or damage while being shipped. Moreover, these products must meet certain cosmetic criteria, be packed in uniform size and in standard containers to facilitate transactions between the packer or broker and the wholesaler who buys the produce "sight unseen." Finally, elaborate processing or chemical tech-

nologies are often needed to guarantee the continual availability and extra shelf life of many products.

There have been two results of this national distribution system. First, consumers have become accustomed to, and have come to expect, a variety of fresh produce all year long. Second, certain states with virtually a year-round growing season have gradually come to dominate certain food sectors, eliminating other agricultural regions from the market for those products.

For the past 10 years, American consumers have seen a rapid increase in food prices. According to the Bureau of Labor Statistics in Washington, food price levels increased 57% from 1970 to 1976. Eighty-seven percent of that increase was caused by higher costs associated with *marketing* the food. These costs include off-farm labor, packaging, machinery, transportation, advertising, energy expenses, and profits. Labor is the largest food marketing cost, comprising 51% of the total food marketing bill. But transportation and profits are increasing at a more rapid rate.

Even though Americans are spending more money for their food, farm incomes are not increasing proportionately. On the average, for every dollar consumers spend on food, farmers receive 31 cents. The remaining 69 cents go to the food processing and marketing industries. The more processed a product, of course, the lower the percentage received by the farmer. For example, out of a dollar a consumer spends on white bread (a highly processed product) farmers receive only 12 cents. A much less processed product, such as lettuce, returns 30 cents to farmers, leaving 70 cents for marketing. Eggs give farmers 65 cents out of a consumer's dollar.

At the same time, farm production costs continue to escalate. Since 1959, farm production expenses have tripled, while net farm income has only doubled. During the 1950-1975 period, this country saw half of its farms disappear, as farmers either got bigger or got out.

Direct Marketing Is Attractive Again

In this situation of rising food costs and declining farm incomes, many communities are experimenting with alternate food distribution systems. This has caused a modest resurgence in direct marketing. Other factors also contribute to the new popularity of direct marketing.

First is a growing concern for more nutritious food. In our national marketing pattern, produce must be picked before it is fully ripe so it will be able to withstand the journey from a field in Arizona to a retail store in Illinois. Direct marketing allows local farmers to bring in just-picked vine- or tree-ripened food for the local market. The food is fresher and generally tastier.

Second, increasing costs of energy illustrate the dependency our energy- and capital-intensive agricultural sector has had on cheap fuel. We use fuel for our farm machinery. Our chemical insecticides and herbicides are derived from fossil-fuel sources. Large amounts of energy are used to produce synthetic fertilizers. Fuel for transportation and refrigeration is needed to maintain our national supermarket.

Our growing agribusiness industry has transformed diversified agriculture into a great industrial machine that offers cheap food to consumers at the expense of very high energy use. Recent strikes by independent truckers demonstrate clearly the potential havoc inherent in our nationwide distribution system. When the system is crippled, farmers can't move their produce to the wholesale markets and western packers can't ship food to markets in the Midwest and East. Newspapers told the story of a Bakersfield, California farmer who had to plow under $500,000 worth of rotting potatoes because the wholesale market could not distribute them. And a packing company in Salinas, California, reported that it had to plow under 500,000 heads of lettuce.

Third, many states are realizing that their agricultural

sector is being eliminated and their rural communities with it. With increasing rural poverty and high rural unemployment, direct marketing is one way a state can reassert and strengthen its agricultural sector. Pennsylvania's story is a perfect illustration. The Pennsylvania Department of Agriculture established a direct marketing program specifically in response to a decrease in the number of small farmers, particularly dairy farmers. Between 1974 and 1976, 4500 dairy farms went out of business, reducing the state's total of dairy farms from 22,000 to 17,500. Looking at the farming sector as a whole, from 1961 to 1970 in Pennsylvania 32,000 farms went out of business and 2.1 million acres of farmland were removed from production. With so many smaller farmers gone, small food processors were also wiped out, since they could no longer supply the large supermarkets with enough volume and variety.

In embarking on an ambitious—and very successful—direct marketing program, the Pennsylvania Department of Agriculture set out to help rural areas which had been under-capitalized for years. The Department estimates that, for every dollar that reaches a farmer through direct marketing, three more are generated within the farm economy and seven more within the rural economy as a whole.

New York offers another illustration of a state reasserting its agricultural sector. During 1975 there was a national boycott of non-union California lettuce and grapes. Many stores participated in the boycott. But some stores in New York refused to stock *any* lettuce and grapes, not realizing those items were also being grown in New York state and not subject to the boycott. This concerned the state agriculture department, which responded by initiating an extensive direct marketing program, along with a creative "Buy Local" campaign to encourage purchase of food grown in the state. Since then other states have developed similar and different programs to encourage in-state marketing. The Kansas Department of Agriculture, for example, has special direct marketing activities designed to promote the sale of Kansas apples.

The Benefits of Direct Marketing

Many people want to know how direct marketing will help them. To a certain extent, the answer depends on whether the asker is a producer or consumer, although many of the benefits from direct marketing are shared by the entire community.

For farmers, direct marketing can be very attractive as a way to increase income. By selling directly to consumers, producers can retain a portion of the marketing costs as income. But in some cases they also reduce *production* costs, because many of the packaging, transportation, and other handling requirements associated with nationwide marketing are either omitted or reduced. Total sales can also be increased because direct marketing provides a market for goods that would not otherwise be marketed. For example, direct market channels are natural outlets for surplus, not cosmetically perfect, low-volume, or specialty produce. Many people, such as home canners, are unconcerned with the size of the product they buy. These people are happy to pay reduced prices for off-size products that farmers cannot market through traditional channels. Therefore direct marketing is a critical source of revenue for small growers whose other marketing alternatives are limited.

Direct marketing also offers producers much more market power and freedom than they have in the traditional marketplace. By using direct marketing channels, growers enlarge their set of alternatives, and therefore can improve their bargaining position in the traditional market. Once producers have the option of selling directly to consumers, they become price-setters rather than price-takers. Furthermore, it is the growers who determine the size and nature of any promotional expenditures, and it is they who decide what marketing services are provided.

Moreover, direct marketing provides producers with an immediate cash flow. No longer do they need to wait several weeks to receive payment. This can be particularly helpful for small, low-income producers whose reserve capital is severely limited.

Consumers can benefit from direct marketing in three ways. First, and perhaps most important in these inflationary times, the cost savings realized by reducing the number of formalized marketing stages generally lead to lower consumer prices.

Second, direct marketing increases access to fresher, better-tasting produce. The traditional marketing structure allows produce buyers in Chicago to be confident that their orders of Florida oranges will arrive on a given day and be of a particular size and quality. Thus many products are now picked green and ripened artificially. Through direct marketing the produce is often picked the very day it is sold.

Finally, direct marketing expands the range of food outlets for comparative shopping. Adding direct purchase outlets to traditional retail stores provides consumers with a wider choice of products in terms of price, quality, and variety.

In summary, perhaps the chief benefit from direct marketing as viewed from either a producer or a consumer perspective can be stated in a single word: *control.* The availability of direct marketing options increases both consumer and producer control over the quality, quantity, and price of marketed produce.[2]

It could also be mentioned that direct marketing serves to promote greater understanding between consumers and producers. By providing opportunities for face-to-face contact, direct marketing can promote a dialog between consumers and producers so that each will better comprehend the other's economic situation.

How It Works

Direct marketing can take many forms. Basically there are two types of arrangements. In one consumers come to farms to make purchases. In the other consumers and farmers meet at some convenient location.

The most common forms of the first type are farm trails, U-pick operations, and rent-a-tree agreements. A farm trail has a group of farmers in a certain area pool their resources for advertising and promotional activities and coordinated purchase of marketing supplies. Often the association publishes a map of the area showing the location of each producer. Information on hours of operation, months of production, commodities available, and telephone numbers are generally provided. The farm trail concept, also known as roadside marketing, was developed in the northeastern United States during the 1920s.

U-pick operations are a type of direct marketing where consumers travel to farms to pick the products they want. They are able to select the quality they desire. Generally the price is much lower than in grocery stores because the consumers are providing the labor, the most expensive portion of a marketing bill. A quart of berries costing $1 in a supermarket might sell for as little as 70¢ at a U-pick operation.

Rent-a-tree agreements are a variation of the U-pick form. In this case consumers pay a single fee for the right to harvest one fruit tree completely. Farmers have the responsibility to take care of their orchards and to contact consumers when the fruit is ready. Many producers guarantee a minimum quantity.

Independent roadside stands are probably the most common form of direct marketing. Farmers sell their produce directly to consumers from a stand located either on a farm or on a nearby road. These stands vary from simple tables to air-conditioned permanent structures.

Farmers' markets at central locations comprise the second form of direct marketing. Basically, a farmers' market is a community marketplace where producers gather to sell. These markets may be located in either residential or commercial areas, in rural or urban communities. The chief benefit of this approach is that by gathering many farmers together in one location, more variety can be offered than in a roadside stand or a U-pick operation. These markets are also more convenient for consumers who may have transportation problems, such as poor and elderly persons. Most farmers' markets accept food stamps, which makes them even more attractive to low-income persons.

Some states have developed a special, distinct market called a "certified farmers' market." At such a market only producers certified by the state or county agricultural commissioner may sell. Certification means they may sell only what they have grown; they cannot handle products purchased elsewhere. It assures consumers that they are buying from true farmers rather than peddlers.

Many communities have done innovative things with farmers' markets. In Oakland, California, the West Oakland Food Project decided to organize a farmers' market when Catholic Charities surveyed the community and discovered that the most important concerns of the people were personal economic problems, and that this very poor section had only one supermarket for its 40,000 residents. Members of the community organized a farmers' market and it has had a successful beginning.

In Tennessee and Alabama, the Agricultural Marketing Project has organized food fairs since 1974.[3] These farmers' markets are held in church parking lots. Farmers move to a different site every day of the week. The schedule is well-publicized so consumers will know where the food fair is each day.

In Indiana, the Department of Agriculture has been able to get many local chambers of commerce to sponsor farmers' markets. Although generally it is fruits, vegetables, eggs, and nuts that are sold at the markets, some attract other commodities. In Scranton, Pennsylvania, one farmer has converted his truck into a butcher shop so he can sell meat directly to consumers. Many markets handle milk and other dairy items.

Some markets have organized free demonstrations on canning, freezing, and drying of foods. At the market in Santa Cruz, California, when one sheep farmer comes to sell his wool, he usually includes a spinning and weaving exhibition.

Farmers' markets are not confined to small cities and rural communities. Major cities such as New York, Philadelphia, Baltimore, Miami, and Seattle have successfully operated farmers' markets for years.

Farmers may also sell in bulk directly to retail stores. Usually the smaller retail stores and consumer cooperatives are most open to this arrangement. Bulk sales to retail establishments can be used to move unexpected surplus quickly off the market. Bulk sales by producers can also be made directly to private or government institutions such as schools, hospitals, correctional facilities, or cafeterias for government agencies. In 1978 Representative Mel King introduced a bill in the Massachusetts legislature to create a commission to evaluate the possible benefits of encouraging the purchase of locally grown food by public institutions. Though it did not pass in that session, the bill is a good model for states to examine and perhaps adopt as public policy.

What About Grains and Meats?

Fruits and vegetables are the commodities most often sold through direct marketing. Occasionally one can buy grains, milk, and cheese at farmers' markets in the U.S. —in other parts of the world they are commonly sold through direct marketing. It is quite rare for meats to be sold directly to consumers in this country, probably because the logistics involved in direct marketing of meats are much more difficult than for fruits and vegetables.

Even though meats and grains are not commonly marketed directly to consumers, farmers growing these items have experimented with some alternate marketing channels. Probably the most extensive is the cooperative marketing program of the National Farmers Organization (NFO). In 1956 a group of farmers near Corning, Iowa, made the decision to market collectively. As individuals, they lacked sufficient volume to market their commodities economically. But by combining their output the total quantity was enough to reduce the marketing cost to a reasonable level.

The NFO today is nationwide. Its regional centers function as bargaining agents for farmers. A commodity —grain, dairy products, or meat—is shipped to a central location. NFO then handles the marketing arrangements.

Although the NFO model has had some problems, it remains a good example of farmers with commodities not easily marketed directly joining together to cut their marketing bill through cooperation.

Support Is Available

There are many ways government at all levels can facilitate direct marketing. In 1976 Congress approved the Farmer-to-Consumer Direct Marketing Act. The Act directs the Secretary of Agriculture (USDA) to provide funds to state departments of agriculture and USDA's extension service to support activities related to direct marketing within or among the states. Approved as a two-year program, by the time the Act expired in the fall of 1978, $2 million had been used to fund direct marketing programs in 25 states. The legislation provided the incentive many states needed to begin direct marketing activities.

The Farmer-to-Consumer Direct Marketing Act needs

to be reenacted with adequate funding to support direct marketing in states which have little or none today.[4]

Further, public institutions can be encouraged to purchase locally grown commodities. In Colorado, through the cooperation of the state agriculture department and the state school food service director, farmers inform school districts when they have surplus commodities that they cannot market through conventional channels. A similar program is beginning in Georgia.

The government, at all levels, can use its own buying power to support small, local producers. The USDA Food and Nutrition Service, which oversees food assistance programs (such as the National School Lunch and School Breakfast Programs) has the ability to influence how large amounts of money are spent. It could do more to encourage direct purchases from small farmers.

Other ways government can facilitate direct marketing include the following:

● Loaning or leasing vacant government-owned land in inner-city settings to an appropriate community agency as a farmers' market. Many vacant areas are available as a result of government programs, such as freeway construction or urban renewal.

● Using employment development and training programs (e.g. VISTA and CETA) to develop alternate inner-city food distribution systems.

● Setting up, on a statewide basis, communication networks to let farmers know where their produce is needed, and to let consumers know what is currently available and where. Since the summer of 1976, California's Department of Food and Agriculture has sponsored a toll-free hotline. Consumers can phone for names, addresses, and phone numbers of farmers located near them who have the commodity they wish to purchase. In the first summer, over 2.7 million pounds of produce were sold through hotline contacts.[5] Illinois has recently installed a similar telephone program.

What Churches Can Do

Christians can help promote and facilitate direct marketing in their communities, either as individual families or by organizing support through their churches. They can shop at existing markets and urge friends to do likewise.

Church members who are not farmers can get to know the farmers in their vicinity, by driving out to their farms, learning what their problems are, and inviting farmers to talk to groups in urban churches. If you have U-pick operations or roadside stands in your area, these provide excellent opportunities to become acquainted with growers.

Church parking lots can be prime locations for farmers' markets. They are often situated on well-traveled streets with easy access to surrounding neighborhoods.

Explore other ways you and your congregation can help small farmers and direct marketing.[6]

Together, we can change the food system. We can develop one that is increasingly more equitable for both low-income people and small farmers alike.

Notes

1. *U.S. News and World Report* (August 13, 1979).
2. California Agricultural District Marketing Guide, Department of Consumer Affairs, 1020 N Street, Sacramento, Calif. 95814.
3. For more information, contact Agricultural Marketing Project, 2606 Westwood Dr., Nashville, Tenn. 37204. 615/297-4088. A manual on organizing farmers' markets is available.
4. To learn of U.S. Department of Agriculture assistance and descriptions of funded state programs, write to Jim Toomey, Agricultural Marketing Service, USDA, Washington, D.C. 20520. Ask for "Facts About Farmer to Consumer Direct Marketing" (AMS 575) and "List of Selected Resource Materials on Farmer to Consumer Direct Marketing" (AMS 577).
5. Persons in southern California who are interested in de-

veloping new markets may ask for guidance from the Interfaith Hunger Coalition of Southern California, 5539 W. Pico Blvd., Los Angeles, Calif. 90019. 213/933-5943.
6. A list of private groups and individuals involved in direct marketing is available from the National Family Farm Education Project, 815 15th St. NW, Room 624, Washington, D.C. 20005.

For Discussion

1. Look at the food in your refrigerator and on your shelves; or list everything you ate yesterday. Where did it come from originally? Is there a pattern of a national or international marketplace? Or is it a local or regional marketing system?

2. What forms of direct marketing exist in your area? Centrally located farmers' markets? Roadside stands? U-pick operations? Others? Do you believe purchase prices are reduced in these operations? Or is income to the producers increased? Do producers who market have a right to more income because they now also perform a distribution function?

3. The author says the chief benefit from direct marketing is control. Do you agree?

4. In the discussion at the end of Chapter 8, you were asked to unleash your imagination and think what life would be like if most of what you consumed were produced within 100 miles and your waste were recycled within one mile. Would direct marketing be an important part of that life? Would different people be exercising control than is now the case? How do you feel about the changes implied in your answers?

5. Do you think more direct marketing should be encouraged in your area? If so, can your local church facilitate it? Would you be interested in taking the initiative? (See the notes above for sources of help.)

6. This section has discussed the *manner* of U.S. farming. What is your opinion of the manner in which farming is done in our country? Should we make some changes? If so, who should do what?

Resources

Following are selected organizations, books, and pamphlets/ periodicals related to the concerns of this book. Readers should refer also to publications cited in chapter notes.

General Farm Organizations

American Agriculture Movement, 308 Second St. SE, Washington, D.C. 20003. 202/544-5750. New farm organization which developed from the 1978 farm strike and the movement to enact 100% of parity at the federal level.

American Farm Bureau Federation, 425 13th St. NW, Washington, D.C. 20006. 202/637-0500. Federation of state farm bureaus. Members include farmers and agribusiness firms. The weekly publication is *Farm Bureau News.*

National Farmers Organization, 485 L'Enfant Plaza SW, Washington, D.C. 20024. 202/484-7075. Concentrates on marketing problems and techniques to promote sales of owner-operators' farm products. The monthly magazine is *NFO Reporter.*

National Farmers Union, 1012 14th St. NW, Washington, D.C. 20005. 202/629-9774. Promotes welfare of owner-operator farms. Concerned with developing purchasing power of the world's poor. Organizations in 30 states with own newsletters. *The Washington Newsletter* appears weekly.

National Grange, 1616 H St. NW, Washington, D.C. 20006. 202/628-3507. Family-oriented fraternal farm organization which seeks to improve economic well-being of rural people, serving as legislative force in state and federal capitals, and providing educational programs.

Church-Related Organizations

Bread for the World, 32 Union Sq. E., New York, N.Y. 10003. 212/260-7000. A Christian citizens movement which seeks to influence federal policy on hunger and food concerns, including U.S. farm policy, food aid, grain reserves, international development. Membership includes helpful monthly newsletter and background materials.

Center for Community Organization and Area Development (CENCOAD), 2118 South Summit Ave., Sioux Falls, S.D. 51705. 605/336-5236. Assists citizens and groups in tri-state area (South Dakota, Minnesota, Iowa) with education and support for "developing quality community life." Established by Augustana College.

Commission on Religion in Appalachia (CORA), 864 Weisgarber Road NW, Knoxville, Tenn. 37919. Interdenominational group concerned with the problems and future of the Appalachian region.

Committee on Rural Ministries, American Lutheran Church, c/o Harold Everson, Box 2127, Augustana College, Sioux Falls, S.D. 57102. 605/336-0770. "A rural voice in the ALC." CORM is an advocate and information center on rural concerns and rural ministry, with representatives from most of the ALC's districts.

Interreligious Taskforce on U.S. Food Policy, 110 Maryland Ave. NE, Washington, D.C. 20002. 800/424-7292. Cooperative effort of national Protestant, Roman Catholic, Jewish, and ecumenical agencies. Monitors legislative and administrative developments on all aspects of food policy, including U.S. agriculture, international development assistance, domestic food programs. Publications include *Hunger* and *Food Policy Notes.* Annual membership in Impact at same address brings *Hunger* and food policy *Action Alerts.*

Joint Strategy and Action Committee, Non-Metropolitan Task Force, c/o Osgood Magnuson, 122 W. Franklin Ave., Minneapolis, Minn. 55404. 612/871-8232. Interdenominational agency with special concern for mission of church in town and country. Write for free copy of "Mission Ideas for Congregations in Small Cities, Towns, and Rural Areas."

National Catholic Rural Life Conference, 4625 NW Beaver Drive, Des Moines, Iowa 50322. 515/270-2634. Publishes monthly *Catholic Rural Life* and *Washington Memorandum,* a news-letter offering updates on government policies affecting rural life, farming, and the land. Many Catholic dioceses have rural life offices also.

Prairie People's Institute for Culture and Religion, c/o Jim Sorenson, Rt. 4, Box 67, Mandan, N.D. 58554. 701/663-8162. Seeks to sensitize Great Plains people to their history and environment as means of equipping them for the future. Organizes workshops and training in rural culture and rural ministries. Write for brochure.

Federal Government

House Agriculture Committee, Subcommittee on Family Farms, Rural Development, and Special Studies, 1301 Longworth House Office Building, Washington, D.C. 20515. 202/225-2171.

Senate Agriculture Committee, Subcommittee on Rural Development, 322 Russell Senate Office Building, Washington, D.C. 20510. 202/224-2035.

U.S. Department of Agriculture, 14th St. and Independence Ave. SW, Washington D.C. 20250. Office of Communications, 202/447-2791, for information. Office of Inquiries and Publications for press releases, exhibits, films, publications.

Other Organizations

Agricultural Marketing Project, 2606 Westwood Drive, Nashville, Tenn. 37204. 615/297-4088. Works with direct marketing and appropriate technology for smaller farmers in the Southeast.

Center for Rural Affairs, Box 405, Walhill, Neb. 68067. 402/846-5428. Nonprofit organization concerned with strengthening rural communities and smaller farm operations. Publishes general newsletter (bimonthly), *Small Farm Advocate* (quarterly newsletter), and *New Land Review* (monthly paper). Write for sample copies. Donations welcome.

Earthwork, 3410 19th St., San Francisco, Calif. 94110. 415/626-1266. A center for the study of land and food. Offers films, publications, and consulting and training services.

Emergency Land Fund, 836 Beecher St. SW, Atlanta, Geor. 30310. 404/758-5506. Seeks to prevent loss of land by small farmers, particularly blacks in the South. Consults on farm management in field offices in Alabama and Mississippi—legal services, financial assistance, tax help.

National Family Farm Coalition, 815 15th St. NW, Room 624, Washington, D.C. 20005. 202/638-6848. Coordinates information and public education around the issues of the Family Farm Development Act, pending in Congress since 1978.

National Land for People, 2348 N. Cornelia, Fresno, Calif. 93711. Advocacy group concerned with struggle of small farmers for control of land and water resources, especially in California and the West. Membership includes monthly publication *Land, Food, People.*

National Rural Center, 1828 L St. NW, Washington, D.C. 20036. 800/424-9679. Nonprofit organization concerned about rural poverty and participation in decision making by all rural people. Develops policy alternatives for rural community. Newsletter (rural health and public transportation), issue reports, and telephone inquiries are available free.

National Sharecroppers Fund, 2128 Commonwealth Ave., Charlotte, N.C. 28205. 704/334-3051. Works for passage of national legislation to benefit small farmers and agricultural workers. Supports efforts of farm workers to organize and seeks to end their exclusion from benefits of social legislation.

Rural America, Inc. 1346 Connecticut Ave. NW, Washington, D.C. 20036. 202/659-2800. National membership organization concerned with full scope of rural problems. Promotes program of policy-oriented research and public information. Publications: *Toward a Platform for Rural America; Rural America* (monthly paper).

Small Farm Energy Project, Box 736, Hartington, Neb. 68739. 402/254-6893. National research and demonstration project to assist small farmers in use of low-cost alternative energy systems. Seeks to expand demonstrations beyond Nebraska. Information services (literature, bibliographies) available free.

Books

Anderson, Ronald. *Why Don't They Understand Us?* Colling-wood, Victoria, Australia: Ronald Anderson and Associates. 1979. (A book on how to increase understanding between farm and city people, written by an Australian but with many U.S. examples. Available from Ag World, 1186 W Summer St., St. Paul, Minn. 55113.)

Barnes, Peter, ed. *The People's Land.* Emmaus, Penn.: Rodale Press, 1975. (Comprehensive picture of the American land reform movement. Depicts roots and consequences of own-ership-related problems and concrete proposals for alterna-tive policies and institutions.)

Berry, Wendell. *The Unsettling of America: Culture and Agri-culture.* New York: Avon, 1978. (A poetic and prophetic statement linking environmental concern, retention of fami-lies in farming, and an ethic for public policy in the United States.)

Breimyer, Harold F. *Farm Policy: 13 Essays.* Ames, Iowa: Iowa State University, 1977. (Provocative commentary on the paradoxes in modern American agriculture, by the noted economist who contributed the energy essay [Chapter 8] in this book.)

Brueggemann, Walter. *The Land.* Philadelphia: Fortress, 1977. (Powerful biblical study of ancient Israel's relationship to the land of the covenant. Illuminates crucial issues of our time.)

Cecil, Kathy. *Food from Farmers.* 1978. (A guide to direct mar-keting in northern California. Can be ordered from Earth-work, 3410 19th St., San Francisco, Calif. 94110.)

Jegen, Mary Evelyn, ed. *The Earth Is the Lord's: Essays on Stewardship.* New York: Paulist, 1978. (Christian concern for creation, the food-energy-environment triangle, and options for a sustainable future. A theologically strong, total stew ardship look at earth-care to meet all people's needs.)

Little, Charles E. *Land and Food: The Preservation of U.S. Farmland.* American Land Forum Report No. 1. Washing-ton, D.C.: 1979. (A wide-ranging survey of the problems and possibilities of keeping farmland in farming.)

Merrill, Richard, ed. *Radical Agriculture*. New York: Harper and Row, 1976. (An anthology of articles offering new alternatives in U.S. land use and food production.)

Nelson, Jack. *Hunger for Justice: Politics of Food and Faith*. Maryknoll, N.Y.: Orbis, 1979. (Probes political, economic, and theological dimensions of world hunger in the light of U.S. behavior. Looks at corporate, military, and governmental policies affecting hungry people. Available through offices of Clergy and Laity Concerned.)

_____. *New Directions in Farm, Land, and Food Policies*. Conference on Alternative State and Local Policies, 1901 Q St. NW, Washington, D.C. 20009. (A packed compendium of ideas and resources on forming policies to deal with farm and food problems at local and state levels. A solid 319 pages [8½″ x 11″] of useful information).

Talbot, Ross B., ed. *The World Food Problem and U.S. Food Politics and Policies: 1978*. Ames, Iowa: Iowa State University, 1979. (An anthology with a helpful perspective in introductions to each section. An academic, but most informative, approach.)

Periodicals, Papers, and Pamphlets

Ag World, 1186 W Summer St., St. Paul, Minn. 55113. Monthly magazine on issues affecting U.S. agriculture. Helpful to both farmers and nonfarmers for monitoring societal changes and varied viewpoints about them.

"Changing Character and Structure of American Agriculture: An Overview," staff of the U.S. General Accounting Office, 1978, 152 pp. Analyzes reasons for changes in U.S. agriculture and identifies issues requiring attention by the Congress and the public. Available from GAO, Box 6015, Gaithersburg, Md. 20760.

Ceres, UNIPUB, 650 First Ave., Box 433, Murray Hill Station, New York, N.Y. 10016. Bimonthly publication of the UN Food and Agriculture Organization; reviews international news and views on agriculture and rural development.

"The Family Farm: Can It Be Saved?" 48-page special section of *Engage/Social Action* magazine, October 1978, United Methodist Board of Church and Society. Order from Service Department, 100 Maryland Ave. NE, Washington, D.C. 20002.

"Family Farming and the Common Good" (Hunger No. 7, February 1977) and "The Family Farm Development Act" (Hunger No. 17, March 1979). Two summary statements from the Interreligious Taskforce on U.S. Food Policy, 110 Maryland Ave. NE, Washington, D.C. 20002. 800/424-7292.

Farmers' Statements on World Food Issues: "Farmers Speak on World Hunger" (1975) and "U.S. Farmers Speak on Grain Reserves" (1977). Two messages from consultations of Lutheran farmers. Single copies free from ALC World Hunger, 422 S. Fifth St., Minneapolis, Minn. 55415.

FRAC Guide to the Food Stamp Program (1979) and *FRAC Guide to the National School Lunch and Breakfast Program* (1978). Walks through the two biggest federal food programs. Order from Food Research and Action Center, 2011 Eye St. NW, Washington, D.C. 20006. 202/452-8250.

"Food Prices and Policy," an overview of the current U.S. food price situation, with historical perspectives and trends. One copy free from ESCS Information, U.S. Department of Agriculture, Room 1664-S (B-K), Washington, D.C. 20250.

From Swords to Plowshares, newsletter published by (inter-Mennonite) Task Force on Farm Issues, Box 347, Newton, Kan. 67114. Also of interest and available to non-Mennonites (donation welcomed). Seeks to relate agriculture to the church's peace heritage.

"Preliminary Report of the Presidential Commission on World Hunger," issued December 1979 by the 20-member citizens body named by President Carter in 1978. Includes analysis and recommendations on hunger in the world and what the U.S. national community can do about it. Single copy free from Presidential Commission on Hunger, 734 Jackson Pl., Washington, D.C. 20006. 202/395-3505. Summary and study guide available from Bread for the World, 32 Union Sq. E., New York, N.Y. 10003.

"The Progressive Land Tax: A Discussion," by Byron L. Dorgan, North Dakota Tax Commissioner, April 1978. A proposal for consideration of a graduated tax on farmland. Single copy free from North Dakota Tax Commissioner, State Capitol, Bismarck, N.D. 58505. 701/224-2770.

"Public Policy and the Changing Structure of American Agriculture," Peter M. Emerson, Congressional Budget Office, Washington, D.C. 1978. A useful 70-page overview of the effects of federal policy on U.S. farm structure. Order from Superintendent of Documents, Government Printing Office, Washington, D.C. 20548.

Sojourners magazine issue of "Land: Who Owns the Earth?" (November 1979). Five articles on biblical and contemporary issues in land control and use. Order from Sojourners, 1309 L St. NW, Washington, D.C. 20005.

"Status of the Family Farm: Second Annual Report to Congress," Ag. Economic Report No. 434. One copy free from ESCS Publications, Room 0054, USDA South Building, Washington, D.C. 20250. 202/447-7255.

"Strangers and Guests: Toward Community in the Heartland," a study statement on land from the Roman Catholic bishops of 12 midwestern states. Single copies free from diocesan rural life office or bishop.

"Structure Issues of American Agriculture," a background document for the hearings on the structure of U.S. agriculture conducted by Secretary Bob Bergland in November-December 1979. One copy free from ESCS Publications, Room 0054-S, USDA South Building, Washington, D.C. 20250.

"What Causes Food Prices to Rise? What Can Be Done About It?" General Accounting Office, 1978. Order from GAO, Box 6015, Gaithersburg, Md. 20760. Single copy free.

"Who Owns the Land?" The preliminary report of a U.S. land ownership survey by the Department of Agriculture. 21 pages of charts, statistics, and summary findings. One copy free from ESCS Publications, Room 0054, USDA South Building, Washington, D.C. 20250.

Denominational Statements

(see the list on p. 76 of this book)